Visitron: the Language of Presentations

Handbook

Devised and written by Brian Howe

Brian Howe is a freelance course designer and consultant, specialising in the area of management communication for both non-native and native speakers of English.

Visitron: the Language of Presentations was originally developed by Specialist Language Services (International) Ltd.
At its centre in York, England, Specialist Language Services (International) Ltd runs courses in all aspects of English language communication, as required by managers of international companies.

Longman

Contents

Preface	iii
The objectives of *Visitron: the Language of Presentations*	iii
A note to the course organiser	iii
To the student: How to use this Handbook	iv
Familiarisation Unit: This is Visitron	vi
The competition	viii
Visitron – a company in crisis	ix
Video programme content	x
Unit 1: Starting the presentation	1
Unit 2: Presenting the overview	5
Unit 3: Presenting background information	9
Unit 4: Relating the past to the present	13
Unit 5: Presenting diagrams	17
Unit 6: Describing markets	21
Unit 7: Describing the financial situation	25
Unit 8: Interpreting the evidence	29
Unit 9: Getting to the heart of the matter	33
Unit 10: Turning to the future	37
Unit 11: Presenting options – 1	41
Unit 12: Presenting options – 2	45
Unit 13: Presenting recommendations	49
Unit 14: Ending the presentation	53
Questions and answers: language analysis index	57
Some practical tips on giving presentations	60
Glossary	62
Tapescript	65

Preface

Presentations are today a key element in international management communication. Information and ideas that were once communicated through lengthy chains of meetings or memoranda are now presented by the person responsible at carefully structured sessions where a chosen audience can listen and respond directly. The benefits are clear. A presentation is a performance. It concentrates the mind and the energies of the presenter and encourages high receptivity from the audience. It therefore focusses and accelerates information exchange within a company and brings rapid and effective feedback.

Because of such benefits presentation has become a clearly defined management skill. Specialised courses in presentation are now a common feature of management training programmes in most large companies. In international companies where many managers are non-native speakers of English, the language aspects of presentation skills are vitally important. *Visitron: the Language of Presentations* has been developed specifically for such managers and executives.

The objectives of *Visitron: the Language of Presentations*

The *Visitron* package, consisting of two video cassettes, a Teacher's Manual and this Handbook, has been designed to identify, present and practise the key areas of English used in typical business presentations. The programme has two main objectives. Its first aim is to help the non-native manager to construct and deliver presentations in English. Its second aim is to help such managers to participate fully as members of the audience in English-speaking presentations.

A note to the course organiser

This Handbook has been designed for use by the student both during and after a course based on the *Visitron* video programme. It is intended to support and complement the teacher's individual exploitation of the material. It achieves this support role in three general areas. Firstly, it provides preview materials both for the video as a whole and for each unit of the analysis section. Secondly, it provides a permanent source of reference for the student of all the language items presented in the video. Thirdly, it focusses on the key area of questions and answers that is normally an integral part of any presentation.

The Familiarisation Unit on pages vi-ix provides background information about the companies and situations featured in the video presentation. It is intended as a preview of the overall programme for use before viewing begins. The information transfer opportunities within this unit will allow students to familiarise themselves with the background to the presentation and to identify language problems at an early stage.

The main body of this Handbook follows the unit-by-unit sequence of the analysis section of the video. The format and content of each Handbook unit however are designed to meet the pre-viewing and post-viewing needs of the student and not to provide additional material for the viewing stage of the course. The teacher will probably ask the students to keep this book closed during this phase.

Each Handbook unit contains three sections. The first section is the unit preview in which diagrams or other visual items from that unit of the video are provided as a basis for pair work, mini-presentations, prediction activities and general content familiarisation. Any relevant pre-teaching may be carried out at this stage. The second section is the summary and quick reference section. This provides the student with a permanent record and reference source for all the language points presented in the video programme. It will also reduce the amount of note-taking time needed during the course and so improve student concentration during the teaching phase. The model questions included in this section are designed to help the student formulate his or her own questions in any presentation he or she may attend. They are not intended as comprehension questions relating to this particular video. The third section of each unit is the follow-up section. It focusses upon the question and answer skills needed during or after a presentation. It consists of dialogues involving the presenter and his audience in which question and answer forms and techniques are clearly identified. Each dialogue relates either to the business content of that unit or to the language items highlighted in that unit. At the end of each dialogue there is a brief functional analysis of the main language points.

The Handbook concludes with a glossary, some practical tips on giving presentations and the full tapescript of Richard Hamilton's presentation.

To the student

This Handbook is for use with the *Visitron: the Language of Presentations* video package. It contains preview and follow-up materials for use with the video *during* the course. It also contains summaries of all the language points in the video for use *after* the course whenever the student needs to give a presentation in English.

Most non-native managers know the problems of presenting information and ideas in English. Communication is difficult because they have to think about language at the same time as they have to think about ideas. The aim of the *Visitron* video package is to help such managers to identify and practise the English needed in a presentation, so that they can then concentrate on ideas.

What is the typical language of business presentation? Clearly general problems of grammar and vocabulary are as important to managers as they are to other students of English. Managers however will also need to know how to present figures and calculations and how to describe diagrams. They will need to know how to make recommendations and justify decisions. They will need to be able to talk about markets and finance and general business situations. In addition to these areas of English however, managers will need to learn that special area of language that will help them to organise and talk about ideas clearly. 'Let me begin by . . . ' or 'I want to go on to . . .' are examples of those special words and phrases which tell the audience about the plan and direction of a speech or presentation. They are very important for a presenter's confidence. They will help to avoid silences. They will help to join one part of a presentation to another and they will also give the presenter valuable thinking time between those parts. The student will find all these language points clearly identified in the video programme and this Handbook.

How to use this Handbook

The Handbook begins with a familiarisation unit for use before you begin viewing the video programme. This unit contains general information about the company called Visitron, its markets and its competitors. Study the diagrams and newspaper articles in this section, and talk about them with your teacher and your colleagues. Try to present some of the information to your colleagues and ask them questions about the products, companies and locations shown. You could also try to give your opinions about the general problems facing Visitron. When you are familiar with the overall business situation facing Visitron, you will be ready to begin viewing the video.

Units 1–14 of this Handbook

Each unit of this Handbook is for use with the corresponding unit of the analysis section of the video. Each Handbook unit has three sections.

Preview

This section is for use *before* you begin viewing the corresponding unit of the video. Its aim is to give you the background that a member of the audience of such a presentation would often have *before* attending the presentation. At the beginning of this section there are short descriptions of the language and presentation points that will occur in this unit. After this you will find a diagram or picture taken from the video unit itself. Around these diagrams and pictures there is a series of questions. Often you will be able to answer these questions directly from the diagram in front of you. Occasionally however you will only be able to answer them by viewing the video itself. Your teacher will tell you when this is the case.

Summary and quick reference

This is the central section of each unit and is for use *after* your course whenever you need to give or attend a presentation in your job. It contains all the phrases shown in the analysis section of the video and also gives examples of how these phrases can be used with the practice activities in the video. This section also contains some model questions. These are examples of the kinds of questions you can ask in the particular language area under review in that unit. If for example the language area under review is 'Expressing purpose', then the model questions will show you how to ask questions about purpose. The model questions are only examples of questions. They are not intended to be comprehension questions about the video.

Follow-up

This section consists of dialogues from an imaginary question and answer session following the presentation seen on the video. These dialogues do not appear in the video but are designed to help you to construct, answer and understand the kinds of questions that follow a typical presentation. All the key words and phrases are clearly identified both in the dialogues and in a language analysis section after each dialogue.

Some practical tips on giving presentations

On pages 60-61 you will find some step-by-step suggestions on how to construct and deliver a presentation.

Glossary

At the end of this Handbook you will find some short dictionary definitions of the important business words and phrases which appear both in the video presentation and the question and answer dialogues in this Handbook.

Tapescript

On pages 65-68 you will find a complete tapescript of the video presentation.

Audio cassette

There is an audio cassette to accompany the Handbook. It contains the full presentation together with the dialogues from the *Follow-up* section.

Familiarisation Unit

In this unit you will find some general information about Visitron and its competitors. This will help you to understand the general business situation behind the presentation that you will watch in the video.

This is Visitron

The pioneers of medical and industrial scanners.

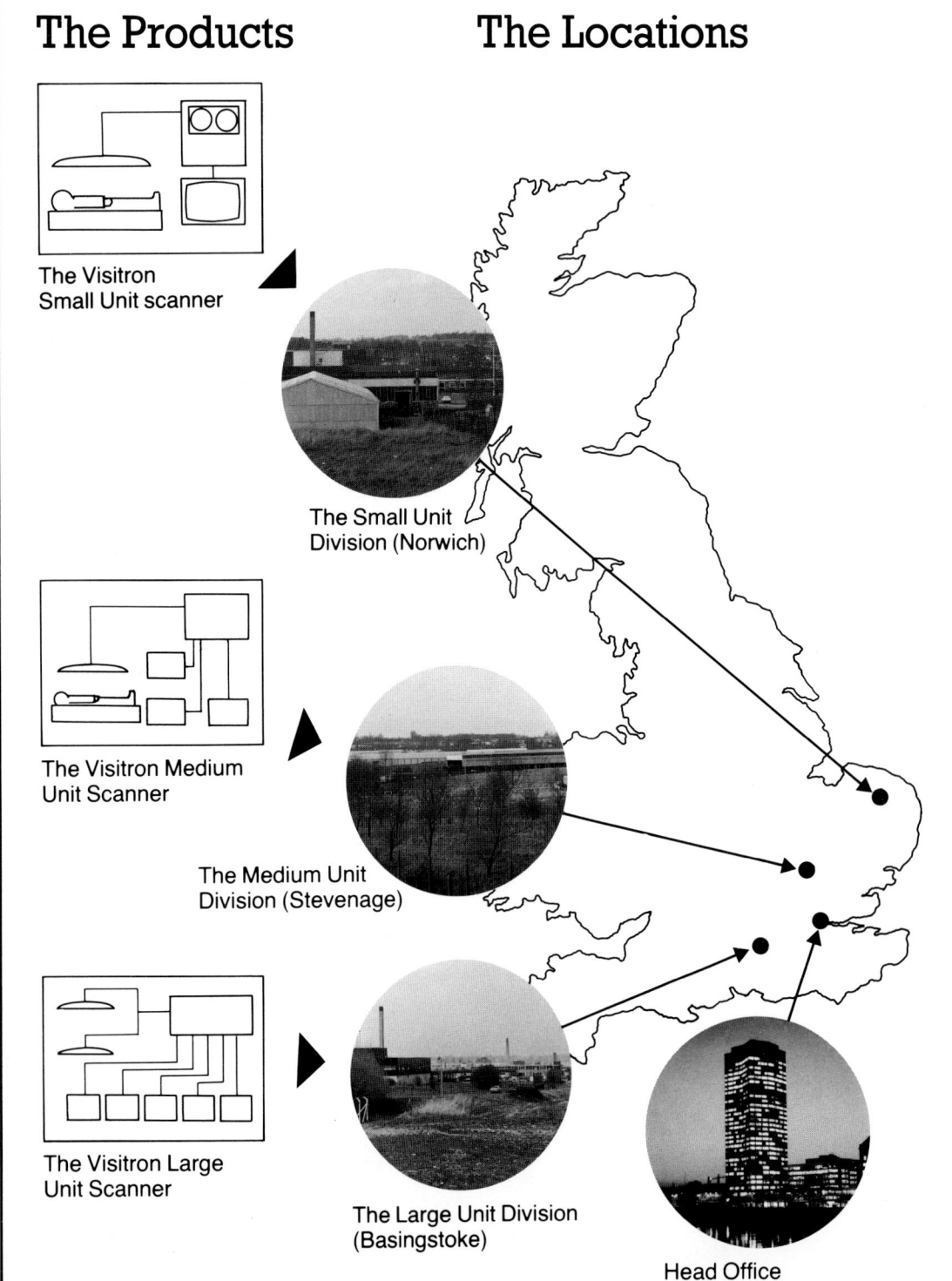

The Products

The Visitron Small Unit scanner

The Visitron Medium Unit Scanner

The Visitron Large Unit Scanner

The Locations

The Small Unit Division (Norwich)

The Medium Unit Division (Stevenage)

The Large Unit Division (Basingstoke)

Head Office (Millbank, London)

The Markets

The Small Unit sector

Doctors' surgeries small clinics

The Medium Unit sector

Medium sized hospitals and engineering companies

The Large Unit sector

Large hospitals and engineering companies

vi

Visitron:
The people

The Workforce:
Total employees = 10, 250

Turnover in 1986 = £212·5m

Pre-Tax Profit in 1986 = £949,000

Stanley Greenstock
The Chief Executive

Robert Scott
Production Director

Derek Lidburn
Financial Director

Jean MacBride
Personnel Director

Sir David Stokes
The Founder and Chairman

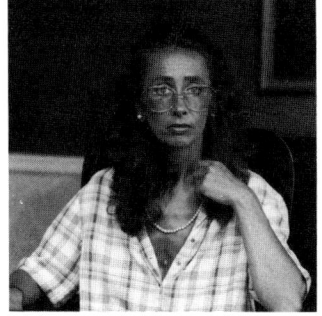

Sheila Appleton
Sales and Marketing Director

The competition

Kamakura K.K.

Chairman
Yasuo Kawamoto

Head Office (Tokyo, Japan)

Factories (Kyoto, Kobe and Okinawa)

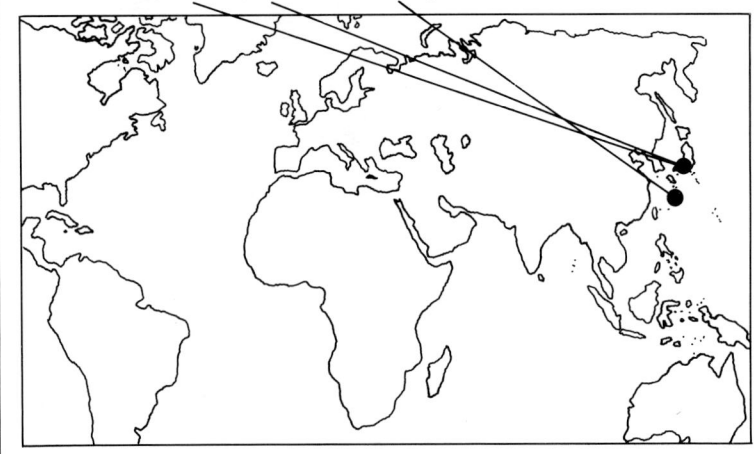

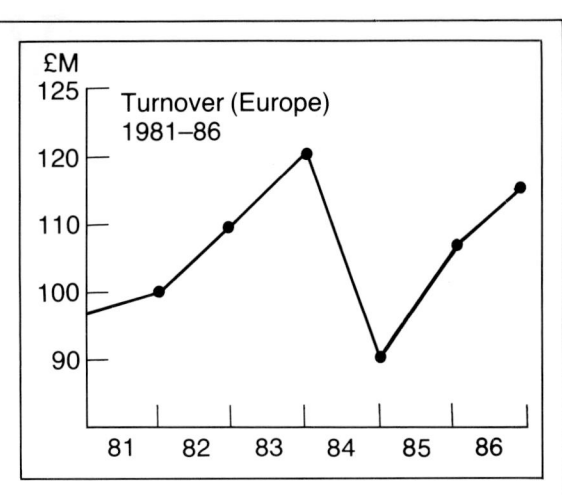

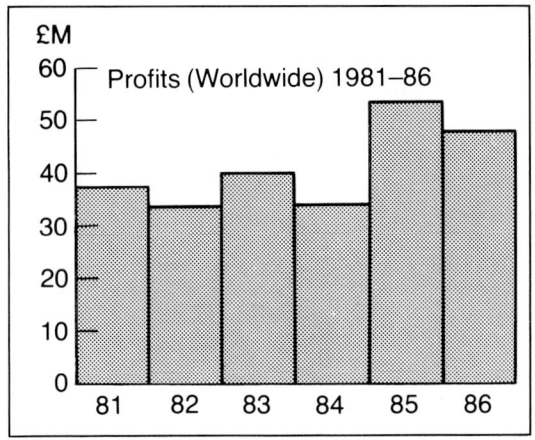

Turnover (Europe) 1981–86 (£M)

Profits (Worldwide) 1981–86 (£M)

Hyperscan Inc.

President
Karl M. Berry Jr.

Head Office (Los Angeles, USA)

Factories (San Jose, Santa Barbara, Stuttgart and Manila)

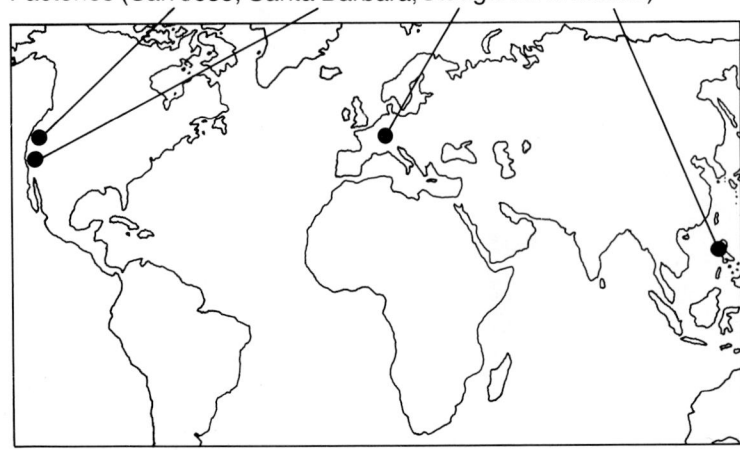

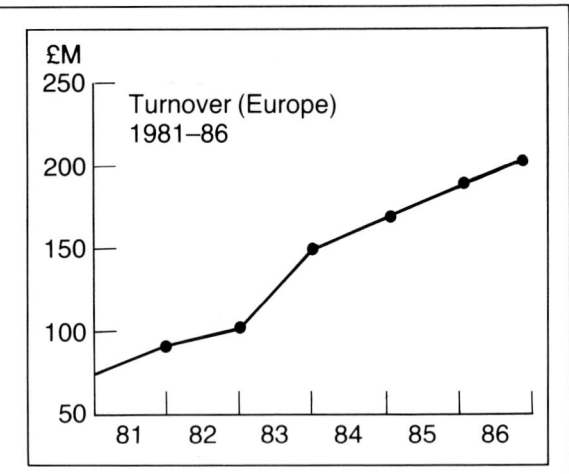

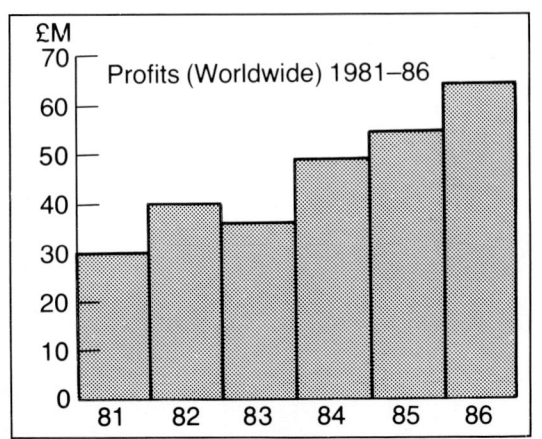

Turnover (Europe) 1981–86 (£M)

Profits (Worldwide) 1981–86 (£M)

Visitron – a company in crisis

The Business Times   December 20th 1986

City News

Visitron shares slump

From our industrial correspondent John Marks

Visitron International, the pioneer of medical and industrial scanners, has reported sharply lower final profits for 1986. Earnings for the year ended fell to an all time low of 2.86p from 5p in 1985. The results caused heavy selling of Visitron shares in an already depressed stock market.

This sharp acceleration in Visitron's decline is due to the latest attack by its main competitor Hyperscan into Visitron's safest and most profitable market sector, the large unit hospitals and engineering companies. In August this year, soon after Hyperscan launched its first Large Unit scanner, Visitron was forced into making changes in its marketing strategy in this sector.

Visitron's poor final figures had been widely expected following warnings in September by Chairman, Sir David Stokes, that earnings would be hit by market conditions. This announcement together with the well publicised calling in of the Smith-Morgan Consultancy caused a severe loss of confidence among dealers. Over 10% of the London-based company's market value was lost in a single day.

Yesterday Visitron's shares were trading at around 178p, down 10p on Friday's close. A company spokesman insisted however that the group was still in a sound financial condition and that the market situation was now under control.

The management column
Edited by Keith Franks

Profile of the Week: Richard Hamilton of Smith-Morgan Consultants

By Ken Donleavy

The recent problems of Visitron International have brought one of Britain's best known business consultants back into the public spotlight. Richard Hamilton, now a senior partner in the Smith-Morgan Consultancy, made his name in 1975 with the rescue of the chemical and paints group Chemtec. Since then he has been involved in several major company turnarounds and organised one of the main corporate mergers of recent years.

Born in Scotland in 1940 and a graduate of Oxford and Harvard Business Schools, Hamilton began his management career with American Business Machines of Chicago. As a Vice-President at the early age of 32, he was well placed to see the effects of world recession on a major international company. It was at this stage of his career that he became an outspoken critic of conventional management consultancy. Companies would not solve their current problems, he argued, by looking inwards at management structures and profit centre organisation. The only way to survive in world recession was to develop overall company strategies to deal with global competition. This meant that companies had to look outwards and Hamilton helped to develop the analytical techniques which are today the standard tools of business consultancy.

Returning to Britain six years ago, Hamilton began to apply his special expertise to companies on this side of the Atlantic. He soon realised that although strategy was still vitally important, there was also the problem of changing the minds and attitudes of large groups of people who control corporate direction in this country. He now believes that problems of 'corporate culture' are often more important in large companies than problems of general strategy. In his quiet but firm manner, Hamilton points out that most business consultants with their high priced, analytical packages almost totally ignore the human and group aspects involved in changing corporate direction. It will be very interesting to see how Hamilton deals with the latest casualty of global competition, the industrial and medical scanning giant, Visitron International.

Video programme content

Unit title	Presentation content	Language points
Unit 1: Starting the presentation	Hamilton is introduced, greets his audience and begins his presentation by setting the scene.	1.1 Signalling the start 1.2 Introducing people 1.3 Setting the scene
Unit 2: Presenting the overview	Hamilton tells his audience why he is there and presents the structure of his presentation. He then introduces his first topic.	2.1 Expressing purpose 2.2 Sequencing and listing 2.3 Introducing topics
Unit 3: Presenting background information	Hamilton introduces his first visual aid, talks about Visitron's past and identifies the factors behind its success.	3.1 Introducing evidence 3.2 Linking cause and effect 3.3 Talking about the past
Unit 4: Relating the past to the present	Using his visual aid, Hamilton points to some surprising circumstances and then brings his review up to the present.	4.1 Directing attention 4.2 Contrasting circumstances 4.3 Relating past to present
Unit 5: Presenting diagrams	Hamilton introduces another diagram, describes its structure and explains its contents.	5.1 Choosing diagrams 5.2 Naming parts of diagrams 5.3 Explaining diagrams
Unit 6: Describing markets	Hamilton describes the present market situation, compares Visitron's shares with its competitors' and looks ahead.	6.1 Describing markets 6.2 Forecasting 6.3 Comparing and contrasting
Unit 7: Describing the financial situation	Hamilton moves on to look at the profit and loss situation for each Visitron division.	7.1 Moving on and looking back 7.2 Referring 7.3 Discussing profit and loss
Unit 8: Interpreting the evidence	Hamilton gives some opinions on the basis of the evidence he has presented so far. He also anticipates a later point by way of a digression.	8.1 Expressing opinions 8.2 Interpreting information 8.3 Digressing
Unit 9: Getting to the heart of the matter	Hamilton summarises his argument so far, identifies the underlying cause of the company's problems and shows the changes that must be made.	9.1 Warning 9.2 Reinforcing a point 9.3 Getting to the point

Unit title	Presentation content	Language points
Unit 10: Turning to the future	Hamilton outlines the types of strategies needed in the future and presents targets.	10.1 Using rhetorical questions 10.2 Disagreeing 10.3 Presenting targets
Unit 11: Presenting options – 1	Hamilton introduces a diagram which shows the strategic options open to Visitron. He then reviews the first option.	11.1 Expressing hypothesis 11.2 Developing the argument – 1 11.3 Presenting calculations
Unit 12: Presenting options – 2	Hamilton points to a central weakness in Visitron's product range and presents the remaining options.	12.1 Prescribing and predicting 12.2 Developing the argument – 2 12.3 Choosing to choose? (Infinitive or *-ing* form)
Unit 13: Presenting recommendations	Hamilton eliminates one of the options he has just described and then presents and justifies his recommendations.	13.1 Justifying decisions 13.2 Eliminating alternatives 13.3 Making recommendations
Unit 14: Ending the presentation	Hamilton sums up, concludes with a challenge to his audience and then invites questions.	14.1 Summing up 14.2 Concluding 14.3 Closing

To Jane, Emma and Robert

UNIT 1
Starting the presentation

Preview

Language points

The Chairman of Visitron introduces Richard Hamilton to his audience and Hamilton begins his presentation.

Signalling the start

Right...
OK...
Right then...

Introducing people

I'd like to introduce...
May I introduce...

Setting the scene

Briefly...
To put it briefly...

Presentation points and preview questions

The Chairman of Visitron introduces Hamilton and gives some very brief background details. Hamilton then greets his audience and begins his presentation. The company's situation is serious and Hamilton knows that his audience will want solutions and not entertainment. He therefore uses a careful, serious and businesslike approach to his subject. He begins by describing his terms of reference i.e. what he has been asked to do. He then sets the scene with a short description of the present business situation.

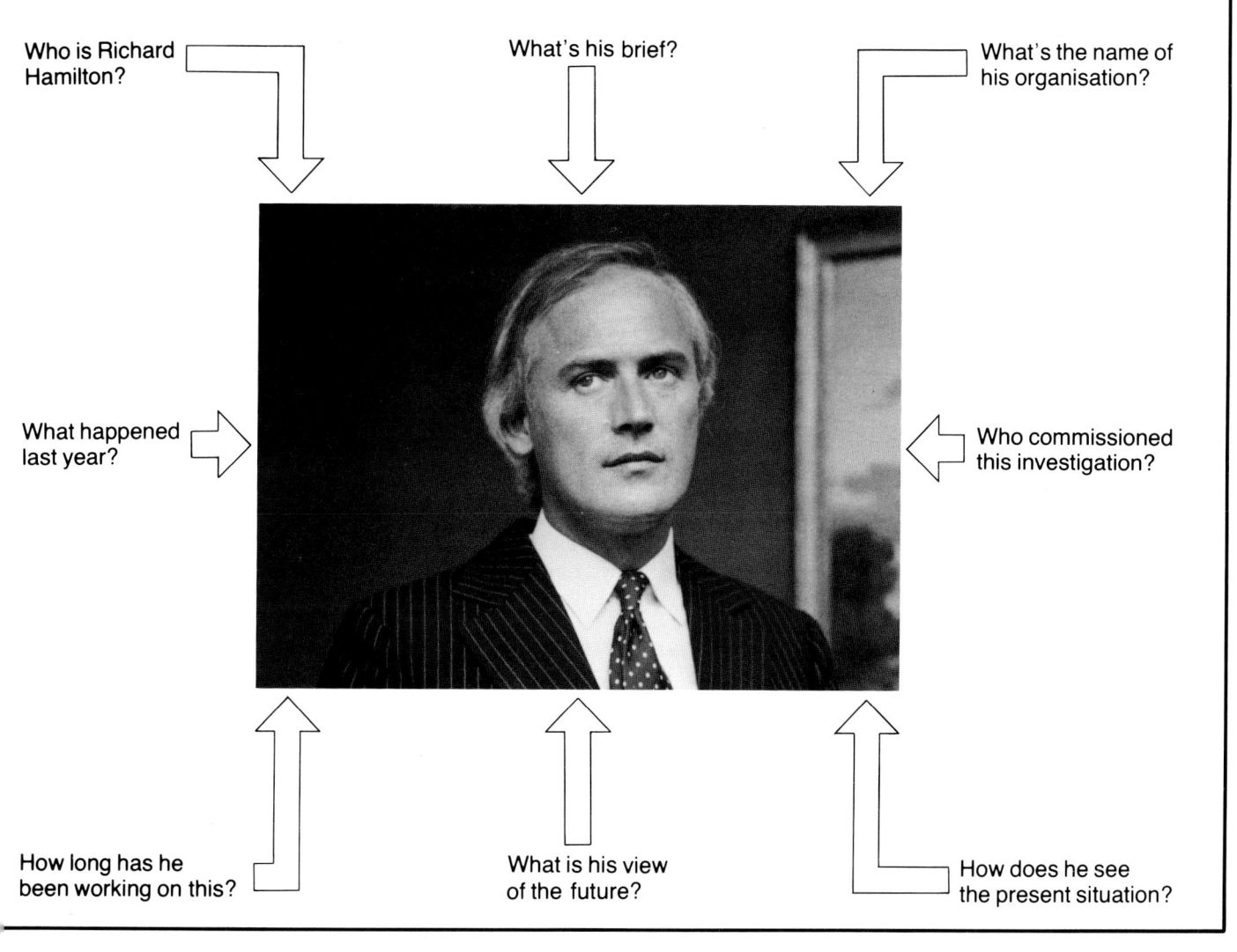

- Who is Richard Hamilton?
- What's his brief?
- What's the name of his organisation?
- What happened last year?
- Who commissioned this investigation?
- How long has he been working on this?
- What is his view of the future?
- How does he see the present situation?

1

Summary and quick reference

1.1 Signalling the start

Right Right then Good. OK So	ladies and gentlemen, gentlemen, everybody, everyone, Richard,	shall we begin?

1.2 Introducing people

I'd like to introduce May I introduce Let me introduce This is	Richard Hamilton.	He's from the Smith-Morgan Consultancy.
I'd like to introduce myself. Let me introduce myself.	My name is Richard Hamilton	and I am from the Smith-Morgan Consultancy.

1.3 Setting the scene

Briefly To put it briefly In a sentence To put it simply In a nutshell	Visitron's initial successes with the new scanner range have not been sustained this year.

1.1 Examples from the video

Right then . . . I'd like to talk about this year's results.

[Diagram: "Let me begin by looking at profit" stacked above "I'd like to talk about this year's results"]

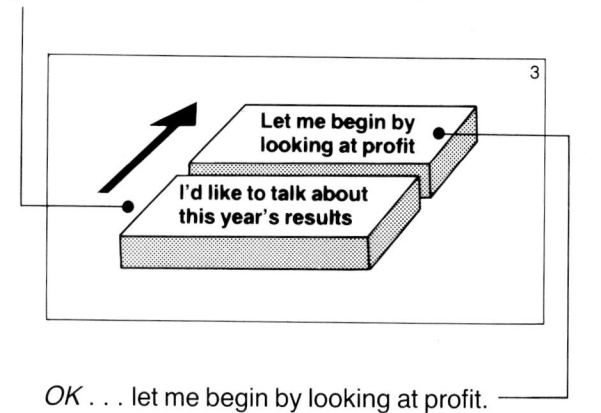

OK . . . let me begin by looking at profit.

Model questions: asking about starting

Are we ready to begin?
Right. Is everyone ready?
OK. Can we start gentlemen?
Is everyone here?
Can we kick off now please?

1.2 Examples from the video

Stanley, *may I introduce you to* Richard Hamilton

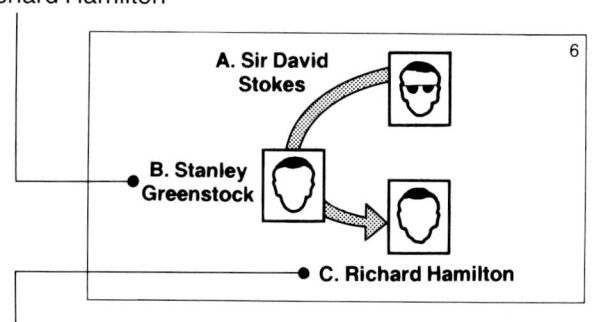

[Diagram:
A. Sir David Stokes
B. Stanley Greenstock
C. Richard Hamilton]

Richard. *Let met introduce you to* Stanley Greenstock, our Chief Executive.

Model questions: questions about introductions

Sorry, I didn't catch your name?
Where did you say you are from?
Which company do you represent?
Which division are you in?

1.3 Examples from the video

[Diagram:
a. £ ⬇
b. U.K. Exports ⬆
c. U.K. Imports ⬇

The Balance of Trade . . . ?]

The pound has fallen, exports have gone up and imports have gone down. *To put it briefly*, the balance of trade has improved considerably.

Model questions: asking about the present situation

What's the situation in the European market?
What's happening to the balance of trade?
How are things with the new product?
What's going on in the Small Unit sector?

Follow-up

Here is an example of the questions and answers which might follow this section of the presentation.

The Financial Director begins the questions

The Financial Director of Visitron, Derek Lidburn, objects to something that Hamilton said at the beginning of his presentation.

LIDBURN: *Er ... perhaps I could begin the questions* Mr Hamilton?
HAMILTON: Certainly ...
LIDBURN: *Could we go back to* something you said at the beginning of your presentation? You described our share price as ... er ... 'dangerously low'. *Don't you think* you're overreacting a little ... especially since the stock market is so depressed?
HAMILTON: *I would agree that* the market is depressed. *Nevertheless* our share price has been falling for over a year now and in our opinion it now undervalues our net worth. The dangers are clear.
LIDBURN: *That may be so* on the basis of net worth. *But surely* any bid would be made on the basis of the book value of our assets?
HAMILTON: *I would say that* any bid would be made on the basis of many different factors. One of them would certainly be book value. *What I was trying to say* however, *was* that the market is worried about Visitron's overall condition and not just one specific factor.
LIDBURN: *Even so Mr* Hamilton, *wouldn't you agree that* as far as the share price is concerned, the condition of the stock market is just as important as the condition of this company?
HAMILTON: *With respect* Mr Lidburn, the exact causes of the present low share value are not so important. *The fact is that* Visitron's share price is over 25 per cent below its 1983 level while the stock exchange index is 20 per cent up over the same period. *In our view* there is a real danger of a strategic acquisition from any number of directions.
LIDBURN: *For example*?
HAMILTON: In the long run acquisition is often a cheaper way of increasing market share than expensive sales and promotions effort ...
LIDBURN: You mean one of our competitors?
HAMILTON: In the present situation anything is possible Mr Lidburn.

Questions and answers: language analysis

The gambits and phrases in italics above are explained below in terms of their communicative functions in the dialogue.

The black arrows represent the people asking the questions and the white arrows the people replying to them.

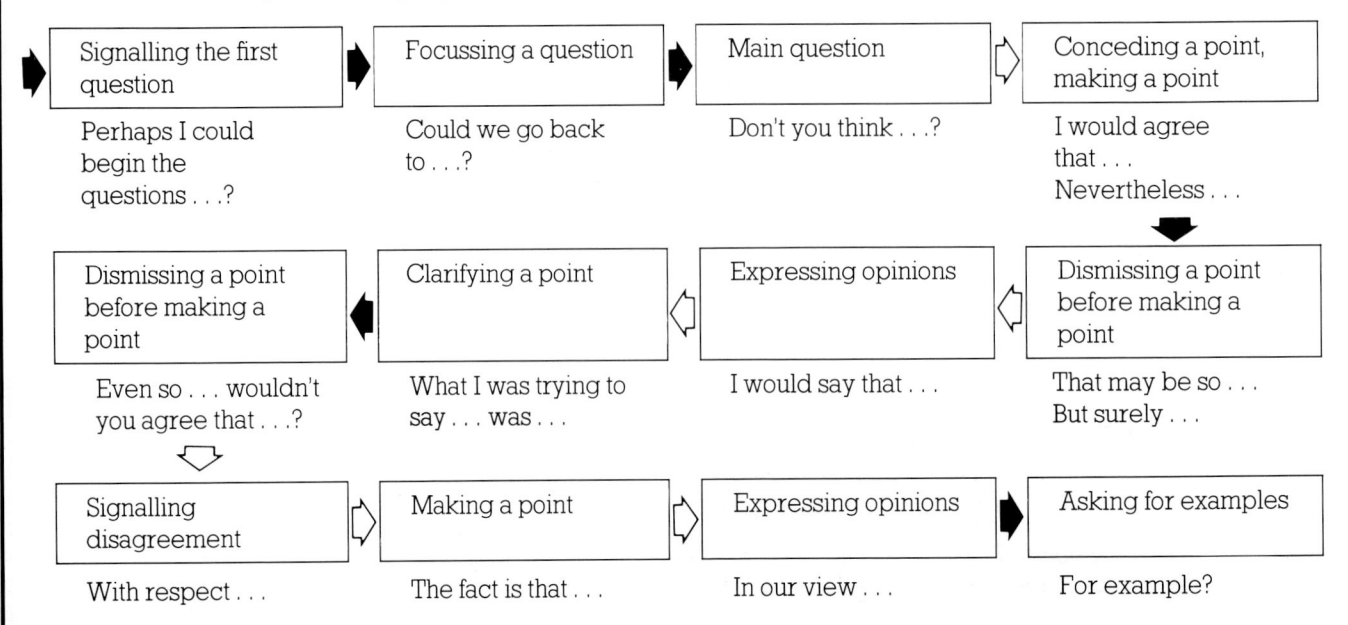

Signalling the first question	Focussing a question	Main question	Conceding a point, making a point
Perhaps I could begin the questions ...?	Could we go back to ...?	Don't you think ...?	I would agree that ... Nevertheless ...

Dismissing a point before making a point	Clarifying a point	Expressing opinions	Dismissing a point before making a point
Even so ... wouldn't you agree that ...?	What I was trying to say ... was ...	I would say that ...	That may be so ... But surely ...

Signalling disagreement	Making a point	Expressing opinions	Asking for examples
With respect ...	The fact is that ...	In our view ...	For example?

UNIT 2
Presenting the overview

Preview

Language points

Hamilton tells his audience why he is there and gives them an overview of the structure of his presentation.

Expressing purpose	*Sequencing and listing*	*Introducing topics*
I'm here today to . . .	Firstly . . .	I'd like to review . . .
My purpose today is . . .	Secondly . . .	I want to discuss . . .
My objective today is . . .	Finally . . .	I'm going to analyse . . .

Presentation points and preview questions

It is not enough for the presenter to have a clear structure and set of aims in his own mind. He must make these clear to his audience also. Hamilton therefore describes his purpose immediately and then gives an overview of the different stages of his presentation. Throughout the presentation he will refer to this structure telling his audience for example when he has finished one part and when he is beginning the next. With such maps and signposts Hamilton demonstrates his control over his subject and his audience has a framework within which to think and respond.

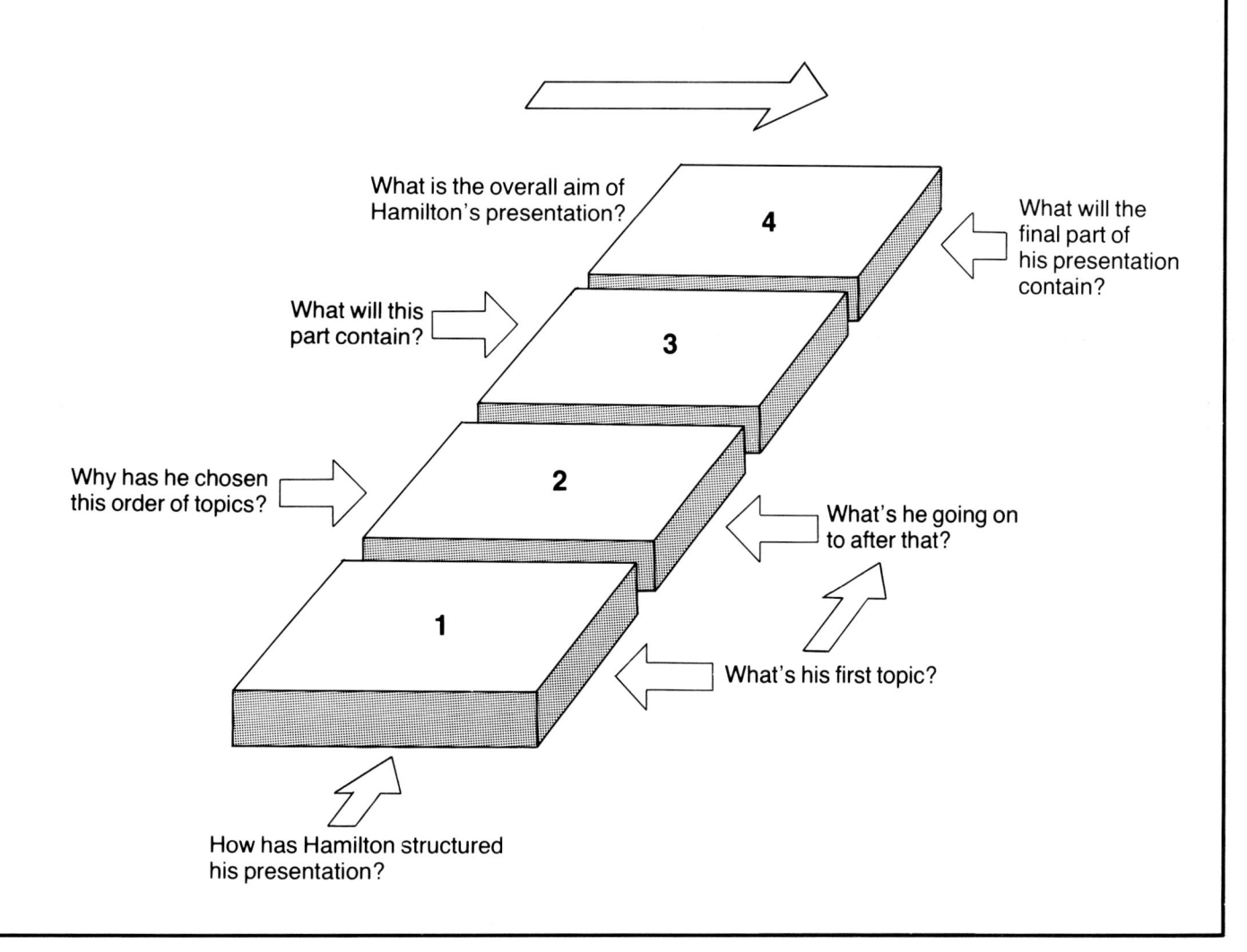

- What is the overall aim of Hamilton's presentation?
- What will the final part of his presentation contain?
- What will this part contain?
- Why has he chosen this order of topics?
- What's he going on to after that?
- What's his first topic?
- How has Hamilton structured his presentation?

Summary and quick reference

2.1 Expressing purpose

I'm here today to My purpose today is to What I want to do today is to My objective today is to My main aim this morning is to My target this afternoon is to	consider the present problem.

2.2 Sequencing and listing

Firstly To start with	I'd like to look at the factors which have influenced our historic performance.
Secondly	I want to analyse the current situation.
Thirdly After this	I'm going to present the options which we see open to us.
Next Then Finally	I shall be recommending a corporate strategy for the 1990s.

2.3 Introducing topics

I'd like to I want to I am going to I shall I shall be	review discuss analyse go over considering	this year's performance.

2.1 Examples from the video

I'm here today to introduce our latest product.

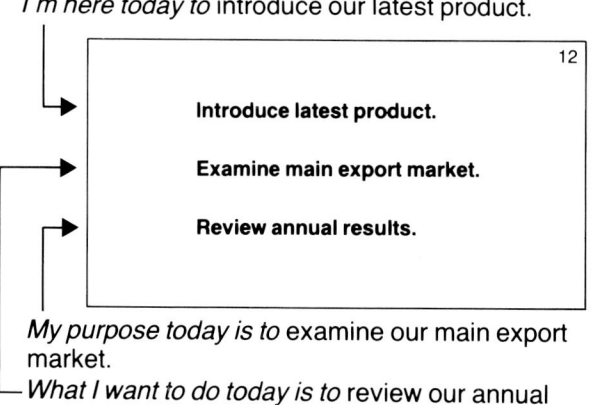

```
                                    12
         Introduce latest product.
         Examine main export market.
         Review annual results.
```

My purpose today is to examine our main export market.
What I want to do today is to review our annual results.

Model questions: asking about purpose

What's the purpose of this meeting?
What's this presentation about?
What are our aims?
What are our objectives today?

2.2 Examples from the video

Thirdly he will be presenting ...
Secondly he is going to review the ...
Firstly he will give his ...

```
                                    18
         1. Historical review
         2. Current situation
         3. Options
         4. Recommendations
         5. Conclusions
```

Fourthly he will be presenting his ...
And finally he will give his ...

Model questions: asking about sequence

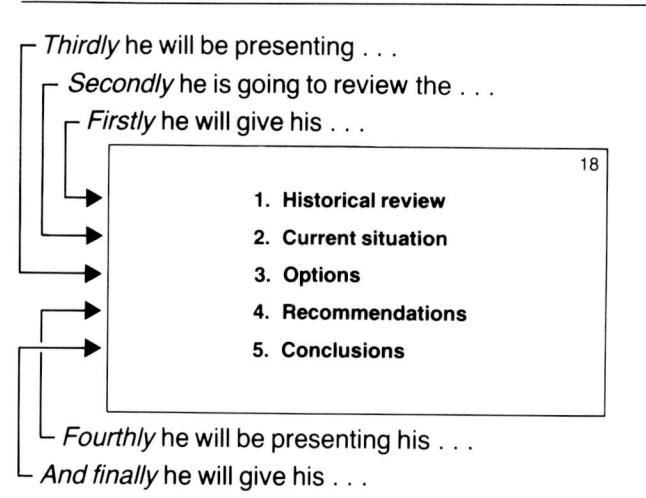

How shall we structure this meeting?
How has he organised his presentation?
In what order shall we deal with these topics?
Where shall we begin?
What shall we do next?

2.3 Examples from the video

Firstly I'd like to look at the ...
Secondly I want to consider ...

```
                                    18
         1. History of my company.
         2. Its present situation.
         3. Our competitors.
         4. The future.
```

After that I shall look at ...
Finally I shall be considering ...

Model questions: asking about topics

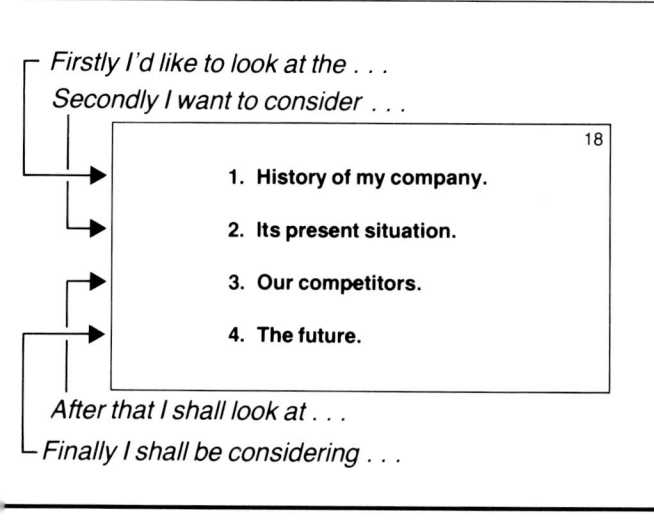

What's the first topic?
Do you think we should discuss X?
What particular aspects of the competition is he going to look at?
Have we covered everything?

Follow-up

Here is an example of the questions and answers which might follow this section of the presentation.

Questions from the Production Director

The Production Director of Visitron, Robert Scott, feels that Hamilton's analysis did not give enough attention to the company's production problems. He therefore asks for more information.

SCOTT: *Could I come in here* Richard?
HAMILTON: Of course.
SCOTT: *It seems to me that* although you presented a very full analysis of our marketing problems, you almost completely ignored the production situation. *What is* your analysis of this situation *and why exactly* do you believe that production within the UK is no longer possible?
HAMILTON: Mm... *I think there are three separate questions there* Mr Scott. *Let me begin with your first point*. Our proposals do in fact contain a detailed analysis of the present production situation. I didn't go into this during my presentation because it's our view that Visitron's major problem is market orientation...
SCOTT: *Yes... but surely* production constraints are an important reason why we have not been able to adapt to market changes?
HAMILTON: *Of course. My point is though that* Visitron must begin by looking at what's happening in the market. After that we can look at the changes that will be needed in production... *Now as far as your second question is concerned*, our analysis of the production situation identified three important weaknesses. *Firstly* the high proportion of labour charges in our product cost, *secondly* the low value added per employee compared with our competitors and *thirdly* the high level of downtime in all three divisions. *With respect to your final question* we did not actually say that production in the UK was no longer possible. We only recommended that Visitron carries out a feasibility study into alternative locations...
SCOTT: Hm... a nod's as good as a wink, Richard.
HAMILTON: *I admit that* on the surface there's a good case for relocation. *However* we need more facts. We cannot make such an important decision without a long, hard look at the benefits... *and* the risks.

Questions and answers: language analysis

The gambits and phrases in italics above are explained below in terms of their communicative functions in the dialogue.

The black arrows represent the people asking the questions and the white arrows the people replying to them.

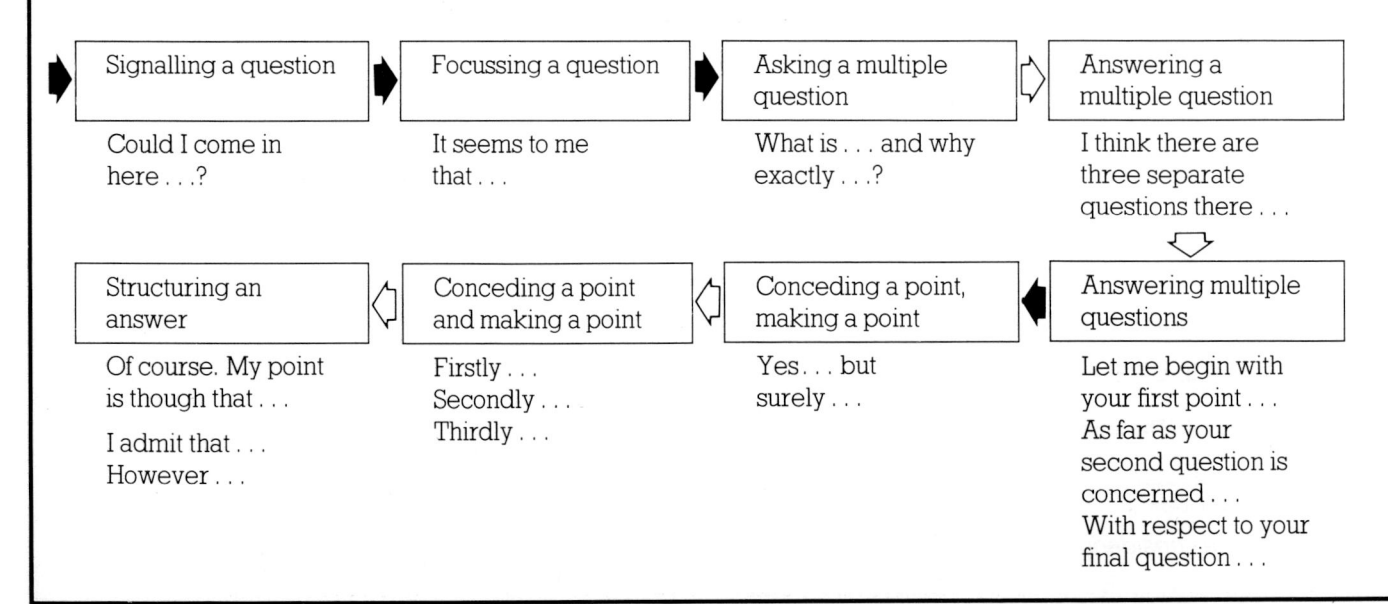

Signalling a question	Focussing a question	Asking a multiple question	Answering a multiple question
Could I come in here...?	It seems to me that...	What is... and why exactly...?	I think there are three separate questions there...

Structuring an answer	Conceding a point and making a point	Conceding a point, making a point	Answering multiple questions
Of course. My point is though that...	Firstly... Secondly... Thirdly...	Yes... but surely...	Let me begin with your first point... As far as your second question is concerned... With respect to your final question...
I admit that... However...			

UNIT 3

Presenting background information

Preview

Language points

Hamilton introduces his first visual aid, talks about Visitron's past and identifies the factors behind its success.

Introducing evidence	*Linking cause and effect*	*Talking about the past*
Have a look at . . .	. . . was due to . . .	Sales went up . . .
I'd like you to look at . . .	. . . led to . . .	Turnover fell . . .
		Profits rose . . .

Presentation points and preview questions

Hamilton's main aim is to analyse the present and make recommendations for the future. To do this, however, he clearly needs to make some reference to the past. In this section of the presentation he puts his ideas into perspective by giving a brief review of Visitron's historical fortunes. To highlight the main points in this review Hamilton has designed a graph which will allow his audience to see the overall situation at a glance.

THE SCANNER MARKET 1961-1986 (1986-1991 PROJECTED): CURRENT £M

Graph labels: £m axis (0–600), Year axis (1960–1990), projection line, areas labelled Visitron, Kamakura, Hyperscan. Annotations on graph: hospital contract, end of patents, 1975 Company Plan, new Hyperscan range launched.

Preview questions around the graph:
- What period does this graph cover?
- What happened to the total market over this period?
- What was Visitron's turnover in 1960?
- What was the result of the 1965 hospital contract?
- When did Kamakura enter the market?
- Why did Hyperscan's share increase after 1982?
- What are the projections to 1990?
- What does he mean by current pounds?

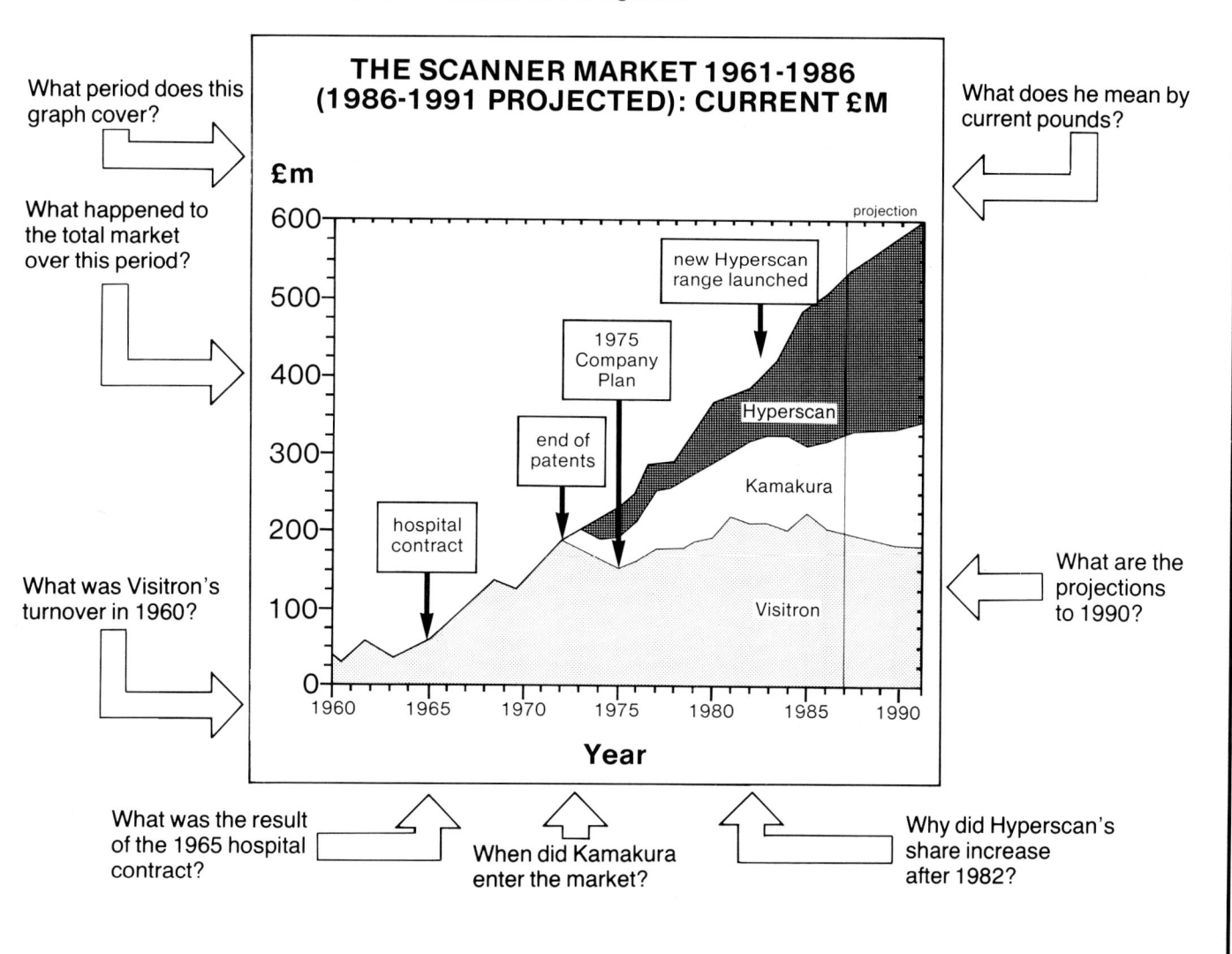

Summary and quick reference

3.1 Introducing evidence

I'd like you to look at	this graph.	
Let me show you	this chart.	
Let's have a look at	this map.	
Have a look at	this model.	
Look at	this matrix.	
If you look at	this diagram,	you will see . . .

3.2 Linking cause and effect

a) Effect to cause:

The rise in sales	was due to	the fall in prices.
The fall in profits	was caused by	high labour costs.
The drop in revenue	was the result of	new competition.
His success	was brought about by	hard work.
His failure	resulted from	bad planning.

b) Cause to effect:

The fall in prices	led to	the rise in sales.
High labour costs	caused	the fall in profits.
New competition	resulted in	the drop in revenue.
Hard work	brought about	his success.
Bad planning	was the reason for	his failure.

3.3 Talking about the past

The Simple Past tense — Actions completed in the past/Actions in a time period now finished.

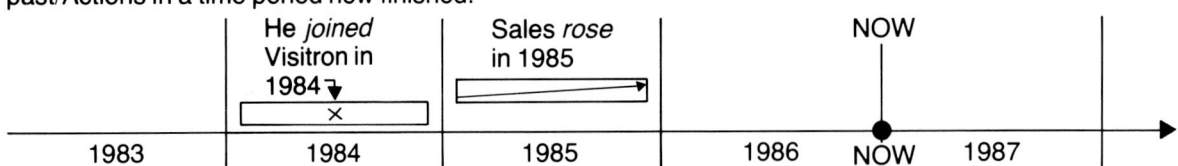

He *joined* Visitron in 1984
Sales *rose* in 1985
NOW

1983 | 1984 | 1985 | 1986 | NOW | 1987

Verbs of	increase	decrease	stability	recovery
Sales	increased. rose. went up. shot up. accelerated. peaked. peaked out.	decreased. fell. went down. dropped. plunged. bottomed out.	stabilised. levelled out. flattened out. steadied. hovered around.	picked up. recovered. improved.
	⬆	⬇	⬌	⤵

3.1 Examples from the video

Let me show you this dictionary?

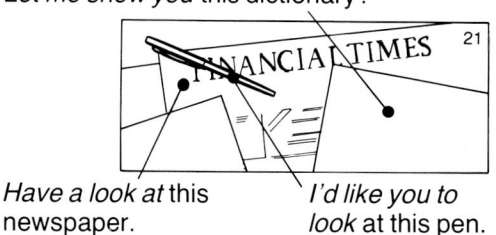

Have a look at this newspaper.

I'd like you to look at this pen.

Model questions: asking about the evidence

Where did you get these figures from?
How reliable are these figures?
What does this graph show?
What conclusions do you draw from this matrix?
What's the relevance of these figures?
What exactly do these figures tell us?

3.2 Examples from the video

The fall in turnover after 1972 *was the result of* the end of patents.

The rise in sales after 1965 *was due to* the UK government contract.

Model questions: asking about cause and effect

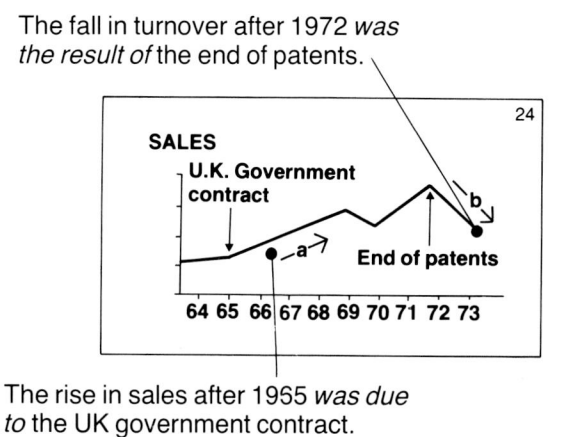

What was the fall in sales due to?
What caused the rise in sales?
What was the cause of the problem?
What was the result of the new competition?
What was the reason for this failure?

3.3 Examples from the video

Profits *rose* in 1982.
Profits *peaked* in 1982.
Profits *fell* to £11m in 1984.
Between 1983 and 1985 profits *dropped* by about £8m.
Profits *picked up* in 1982.

Model questions: asking about the finished past

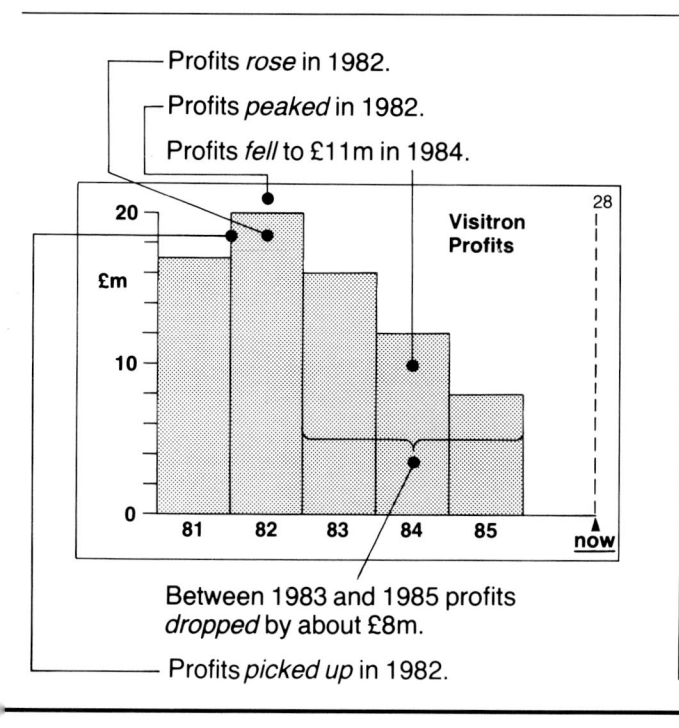

What were our sales figures last year?
Did profits improve in 1982?
Why did profits fall last quarter?
When did competitor Y enter the market?
When did you launch product X?
Who designed the new product range?
What was your market share last year?

Follow-up

Here is an example of the questions and answers which might follow this section of the presentation.

Questions from the Sales and Marketing Director

The Sales and Marketing Director of Visitron, Sheila Appleton, questions Hamilton about the details and contents of his first visual aid, the graph of the scanner market 1960-90.

APPLETON: *Excuse me* Mr Hamilton. *Could we go back to* your first graph for a moment? *I'm . . . er . . . a little worried about* your turnover figures . . .
HAMILTON: Mm . . .
APPLETON: I understand why you measure turnover in current pounds . . . inflation would clearly distort the figures if you used actual values. *My question is whether* this is enough?
HAMILTON: *How do you mean?*
APPLETON: Well . . . did you, for example, take account of exchange rate changes over this period?
HAMILTON: Ah . . . *I see what you're getting at.* No. The figures are based on net sterling receipts.
APPLETON: *But surely* this will exaggerate the fall in the turnover curve on your graph? *What I mean is that* with so much of our business in France and Germany, the recent falls in the mark and franc against the pound will give an artificially low sterling sales figure.
HAMILTON: *I agree* that may be so for France and Germany. In our other markets however currency values rose against the pound and so *overall* exchange rate variations cancelled themselves out.
APPLETON: *OK. Perhaps I'm splitting hairs.* All the same I would prefer to see the unit sales figures rather than sterling values.
HAMILTON: I can quite see your point Mrs Appleton. Unfortunately a graph showing unit sales in all sectors would be extremely complicated.
APPLETON: Perhaps that is my point. Diagrams are sometimes more convenient than accurate. In this case however your figures seem to tally with ours . . .
HAMILTON: I am very relieved to hear it Mrs Appleton . . .

Questions and answers: language analysis

The gambits and phrases in italics above are explained below in terms of their communicative functions in the dialogue.

The black arrows represent the people asking the questions and the white arrows the people replying to them.

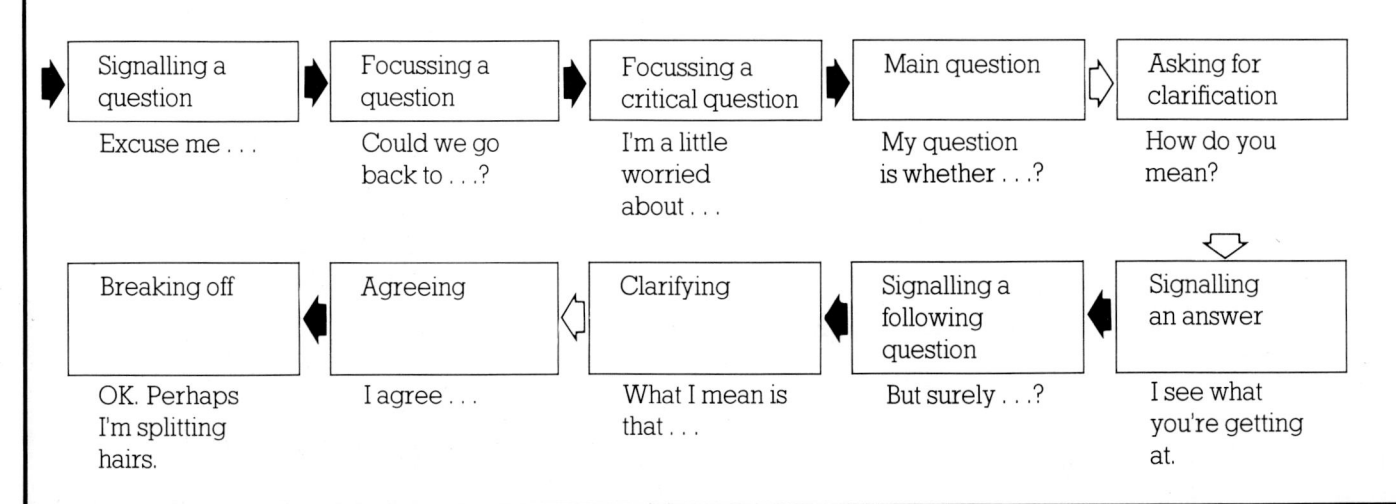

Signalling a question	Focussing a question	Focussing a critical question	Main question	Asking for clarification
Excuse me . . .	Could we go back to . . . ?	I'm a little worried about . . .	My question is whether . . . ?	How do you mean?

Breaking off	Agreeing	Clarifying	Signalling a following question	Signalling an answer
OK. Perhaps I'm splitting hairs.	I agree . . .	What I mean is that . . .	But surely . . . ?	I see what you're getting at.

UNIT 4
Relating the past to the present

Preview

Language points

Using his visual aid, Hamilton points to some surprising circumstances and then brings his review up to the present.

Directing attention

You will note that...
As you can see...

Contrasting circumstances

Although...
Even though...

Relating past to present

Sales have gone up.
Turnover has fallen.
Profits have risen.

Presentation points and preview questions

Hamilton now brings his analysis of Visitron's history up to the present. He compares the scanner market five years ago with the same market today in 1986. From this comparison he draws some conclusions and for the first time introduces some criticisms into his presentation. He supports this criticism with a key management ratio. Hamilton ends this section of his presentation with a rhetorical question. Such questions help to dramatise situations and increase audience attention at key points in a presentation.

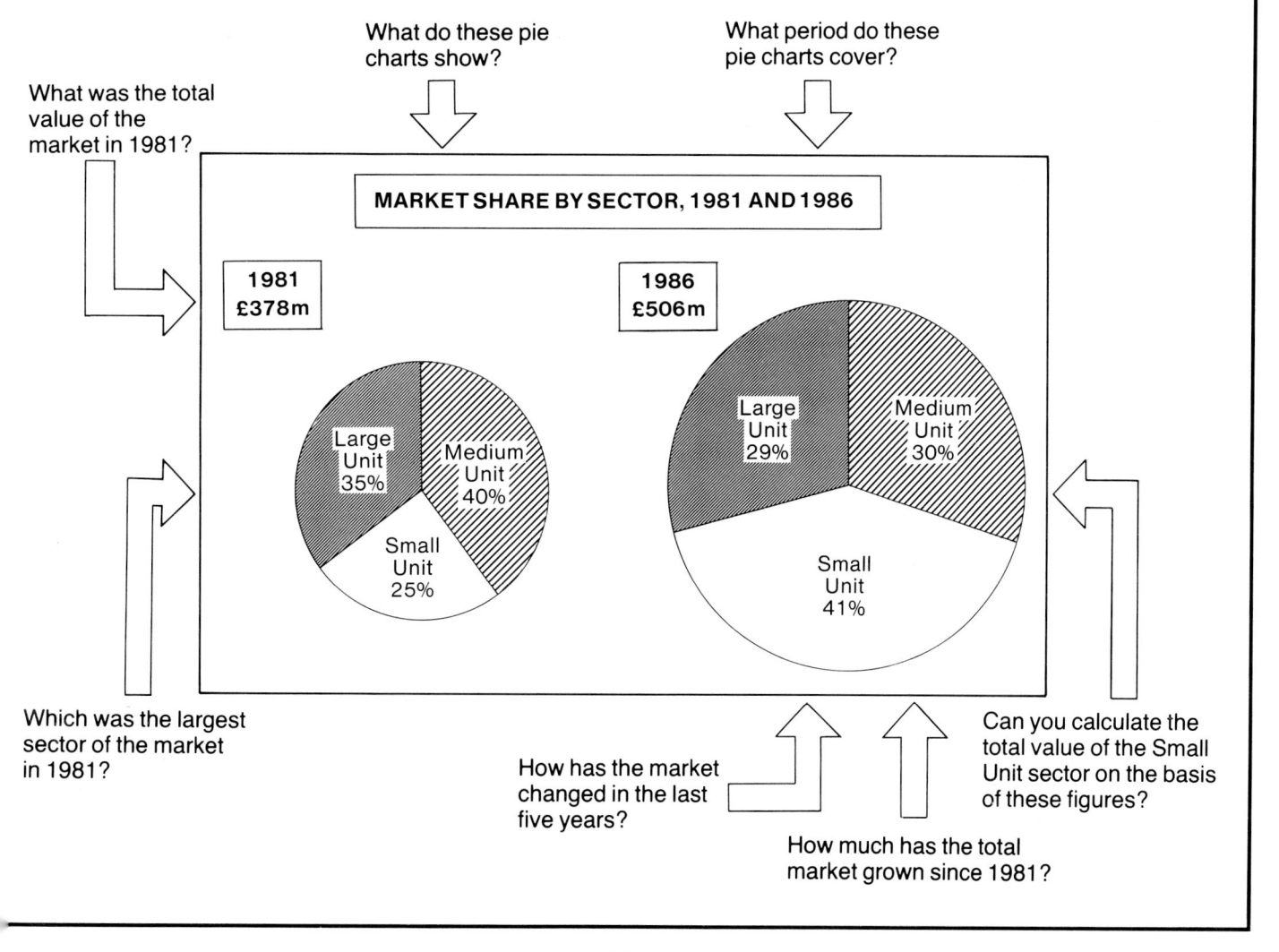

What was the total value of the market in 1981?

What do these pie charts show?

What period do these pie charts cover?

MARKET SHARE BY SECTOR, 1981 AND 1986

1981
£378m

- Large Unit 35%
- Medium Unit 40%
- Small Unit 25%

1986
£506m

- Large Unit 29%
- Medium Unit 30%
- Small Unit 41%

Which was the largest sector of the market in 1981?

How has the market changed in the last five years?

How much has the total market grown since 1981?

Can you calculate the total value of the Small Unit sector on the basis of these figures?

Summary and quick reference

4.1 Directing attention

You will note that As you will notice As you can see As you see You will see immediately that	profits have fallen.

4.2 Contrasting circumstances

Although Even though In spite of the fact that	turnover has increased, profits have fallen.

4.3 Relating past to present

The Present Perfect tense

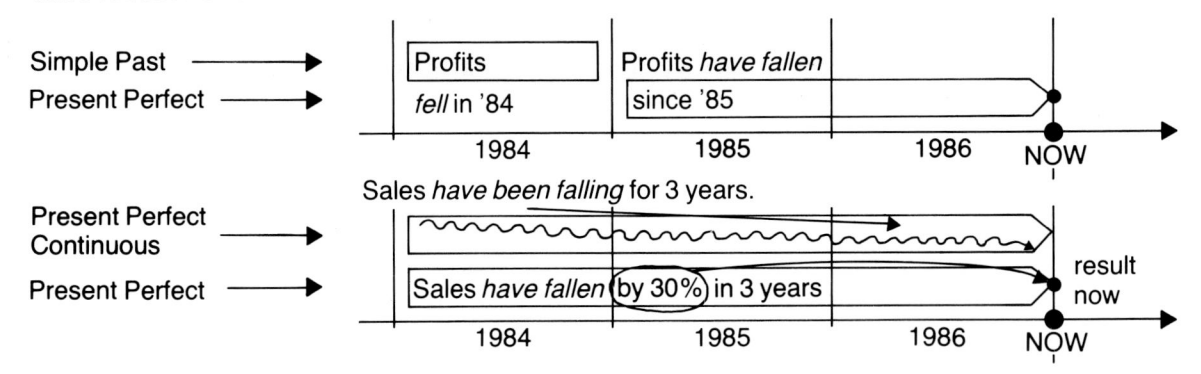

Simple Past ⟶ Profits *fell* in '84
Present Perfect ⟶ Profits *have fallen* since '85

Present Perfect Continuous ⟶ Sales *have been falling* for 3 years.
Present Perfect ⟶ Sales *have fallen* (by 30%) in 3 years — result now

Verbs of	increase	decrease	stability	recovery
Sales	have increased. have risen. have gone up. have shot up. have accelerated. have peaked. have peaked out.	have decreased. have fallen. have gone down. have dropped. have plunged. have bottomed out.	have stabilised. have levelled out. have flattened out. have steadied. have hovered around . . .	have picked up. have recovered. have improved.
Profits	have been rising	have been falling	have been stabilising.	have been picking up.
	⇧	⇩	⇔	⇗

4.1 Examples from the video

As you can see, the patient lies beneath the scanning dish

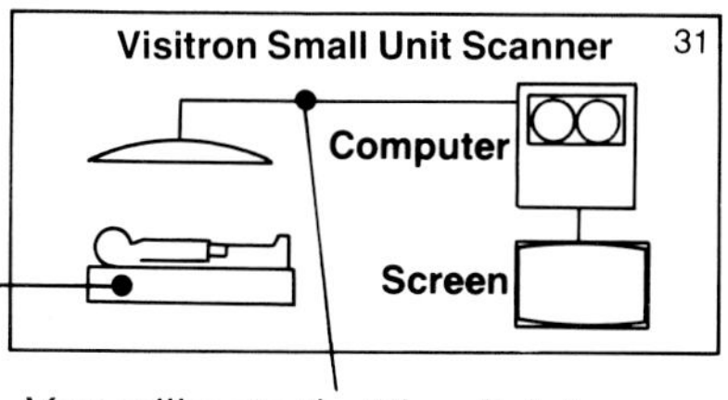

Visitron Small Unit Scanner 31
Computer
Screen

You will note that the dish is connected directly to the computer.

Model questions: asking about features of an object or diagram

What's this component here?
What does this do?
What's the purpose of this?
What's the computer for?
How is the system operated?
What kind of computer is it?

4.2 Examples from the video

I lived in France / speak French   34

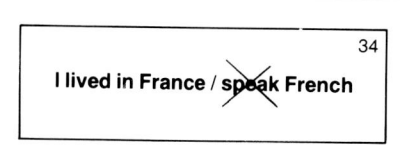

Although I lived in France, I don't speak French.

Model questions: asking about surprising circumstances

Why not?
How do you explain that?
How do you account for this?
Why do you think this happened?

4.3 Examples from the video

Profits *have fallen* by £13m in the last six years.

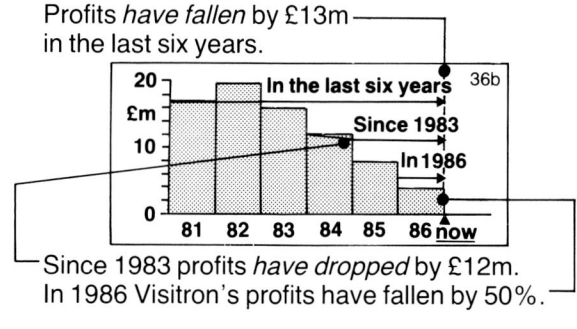

[Bar chart 36b: £m, 1981–86 now, "In the last six years", "Since 1983", "In 1986"]

Since 1983 profits *have dropped* by £12m.
In 1986 Visitron's profits *have fallen* by 50%.

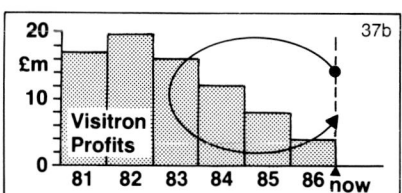

[Bar chart 37b: Visitron Profits, 81–86 now]

What *has gone wrong*?
Why *have* things *got* so bad?
What *has happened* to cause this?

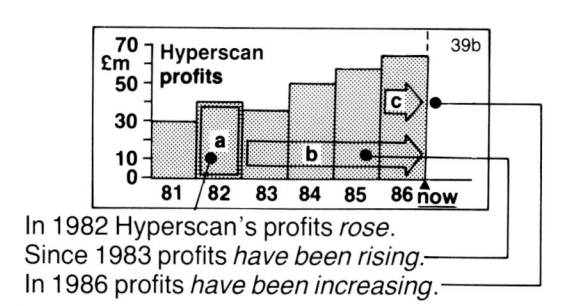

[Bar chart 39b: Hyperscan profits, 81–86 now, points a, b, c]

In 1982 Hyperscan's profits *rose*.
Since 1983 profits *have been rising*.
In 1986 profits *have been increasing*.

Model questions: asking about the past leading to the present

How much have sales fallen in the last two years?
What has happened to profits since 1975?
What has happened to margins this year?
Why has turnover decreased so quickly in the last three years?

What's gone wrong?
Why has this happened?
Where have we gone wrong?

How long have sales been rising?
How long has this been happening?

Follow-up

Here is an example of the questions and answers which might follow this section of the presentation.

Questions from the Sales and Marketing Director

Sheila Appleton asks some further questions.

APPLETON: *While we're on this subject,* Mr Hamilton, *I'd like to ask you about* your sales projections. *Can you tell me how you arrived at* these figures?

HAMILTON: Yes... our projections are based upon an analysis of current demand trends together with an assessment of the producers' ability to react to these trends. *On the demand side* it is clear that customers are looking for lower prices and greater systems flexibility... *something I did not mention earlier is that* the growth of networking systems using the Small Unit scanners is probably affecting sales of the larger scanners... which is another reason for the swing towards the smaller end of the market. *On the supply side* it is clearly the companies which can exploit big productivity advantages who will benefit from such demand trends... Hyperscan will have a large output per man hour edge right up to 1990... the same cannot be said for Visitron.

APPLETON: *Does this also mean that* you expect the Large and Medium Unit sectors to decline?

HAMILTON: *In the short run* we don't expect much change. *In the long run* it is much more difficult to say. A lot depends on the holography research now under way. If this is successful we could see new life in those sectors in the mid-1990s.

APPLETON: And if it fails?

HAMILTON: Then we may have some Large and Medium Unit dinosaurs on our hands...

Questions and answers: language analysis

The gambits and phrases in italics above are explained below in terms of their communicative functions in the dialogue.

The black arrows represent the people asking the questions and the white arrows the people replying to them.

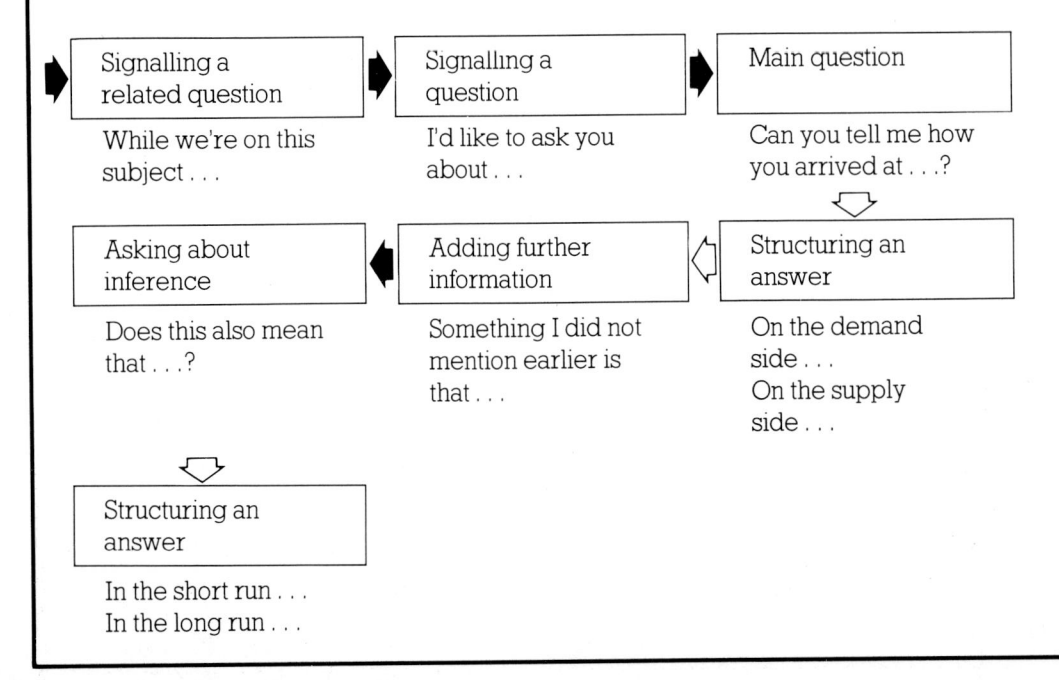

Signalling a related question	Signalling a question	Main question
While we're on this subject...	I'd like to ask you about...	Can you tell me how you arrived at...?

Asking about inference	Adding further information	Structuring an answer
Does this also mean that...?	Something I did not mention earlier is that...	On the demand side... On the supply side...

Structuring an answer
In the short run... In the long run...

UNIT 5
Presenting diagrams

Preview

Language points

Hamilton introduces another diagram, describes its structure and explains its contents.

Choosing diagrams	Naming parts of diagrams	Explaining diagrams
Have a look at this diagram/graph/chart.	The vertical axis represents...	Prices in the Small Unit sector have been falling steadily...

Presentation points and preview questions

Hamilton has chosen and designed his visual aids carefully. Each diagram summarises and supports a key argument or point in his presentation. Each one is carefully positioned within the presentation to give variety and occasional changes of focus to his audience. Each diagram is also as simple and clear as he can make it. They contain no unnecessary information. In this section of the presentation Hamilton demonstrates recent price trends in the scanner market. He takes great care to explain the structure of the diagram before he goes on to explain or interpret its content.

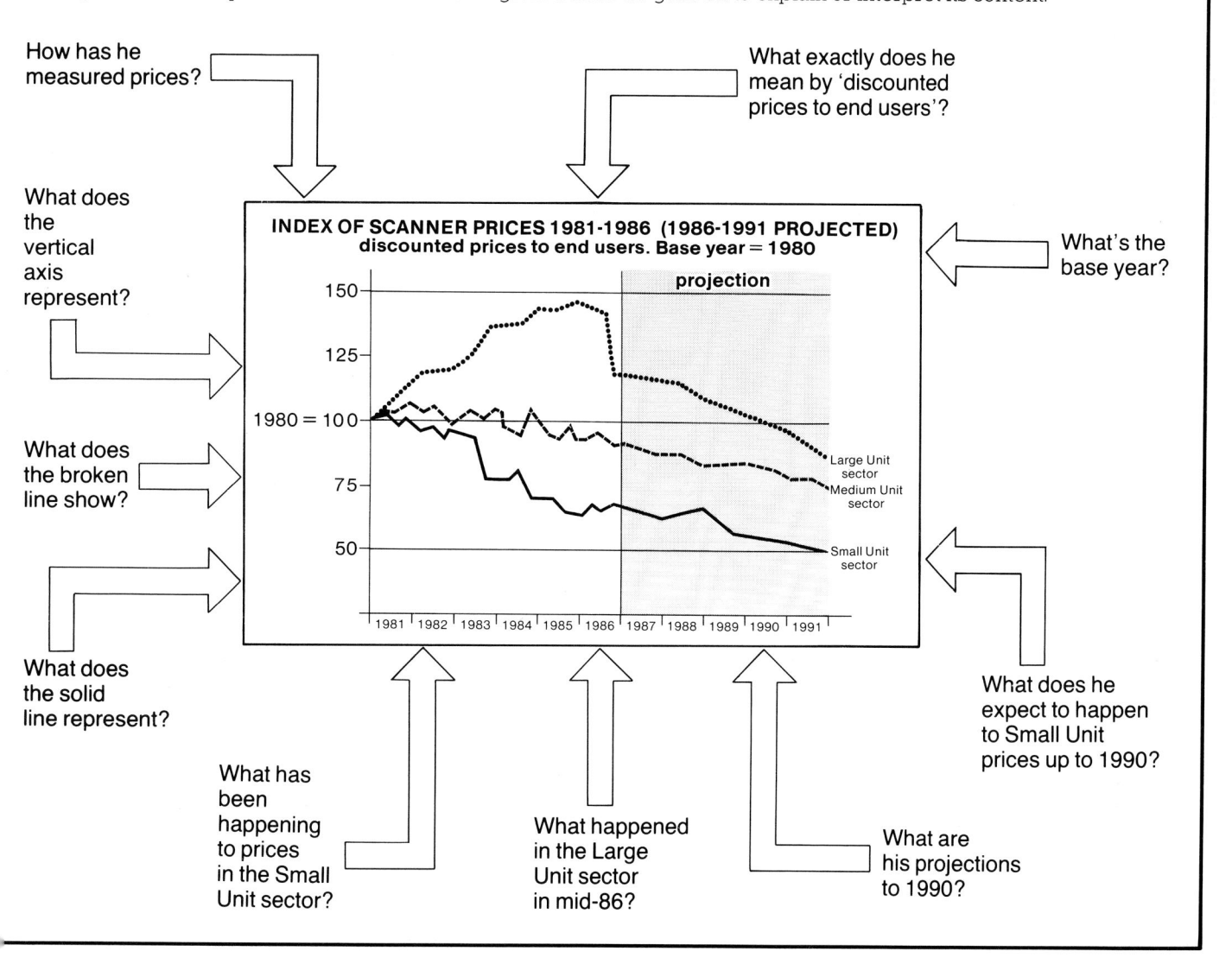

How has he measured prices?

What exactly does he mean by 'discounted prices to end users'?

What does the vertical axis represent?

INDEX OF SCANNER PRICES 1981-1986 (1986-1991 PROJECTED)
discounted prices to end users. Base year = 1980

What's the base year?

What does the broken line show?

What does the solid line represent?

What does he expect to happen to Small Unit prices up to 1990?

What has been happening to prices in the Small Unit sector?

What happened in the Large Unit sector in mid-86?

What are his projections to 1990?

17

Summary and quick reference

5.1 Choosing diagrams

Have a look at		this diagram. this graph. this bar chart. this histogram. this pie chart. this flow chart. this matrix.

5.2 Naming parts of diagrams

The vertical axis The horizontal axis The curve The solid line The broken line The dotted line		represents shows	total annual sales.
The shaded The unshaded The dotted The coloured The red The green	area section quadrant segment column bar	shows	our market share.

5.3 Explaining diagrams

Sales rose		slightly a little gently steadily sharply suddenly quickly rapidly dramatically	in the final quarter of last year.
Profits fell			
After this Following this		sales flattened out.	
At the beginning of In the middle of At the end of In the first quarter of		this year	sales flattened out.
Since then Since the last quarter		sales have flattened out.	

5.1 Examples from the video

A diagram (car with labels: windscreen, roof, wheel, body)
A graph
A bar chart (histogram)
A pie chart
A flow chart (one → two → three → four)
A matrix

Model questions: asking about diagrams

What kind of diagram is this?
What does the graph show?
What period does the graph cover?
Which year does the pie chart represent?

5.2 Examples from the video

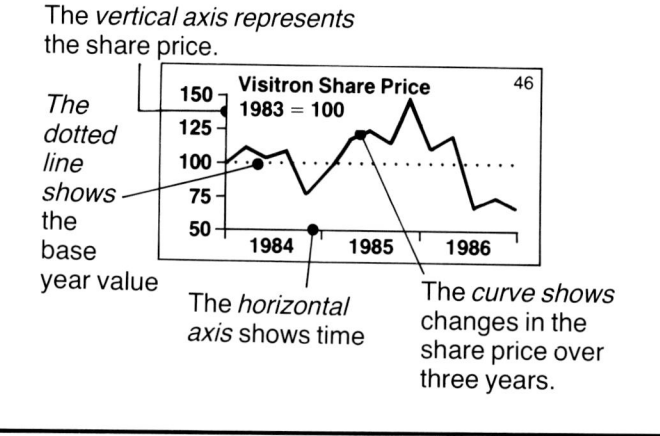

The *vertical axis represents* the share price.
The *dotted line shows* the base year value
The *horizontal axis* shows time
The *curve shows* changes in the share price over three years.

Visitron Share Price 1983 = 100

Model questions: asking about the structure of diagrams

What does the vertical axis represent?
What does the curve show?
What does the dotted line indicate?
What does the horizontal axis show?
What does the shaded segment represent?
What does the unshaded area show?

5.3 Examples from the video

The share price *fell* at the end of '84.
It picked up in December '84 and rose steadily until the middle of '85.
The share price *dropped suddenly* in the middle of '86.
It picked up slightly in the third quarter of '86 but since then has fallen gently.

Visitron Share Price 1983 = 100

Model questions: asking about the contents of diagrams

What happened to X in 1980?
What has happened to Y since 1983?
How do you interpret the fall in Y since 1983?
Why did X fall so suddenly last year?
What was the cause of the rise in Z in 1978?
How long has Z been falling?
What's the significance of the peak in Y in the first quarter?

Follow-up

Here is an example of the questions and answers which might follow this section of the presentation.

Questions from the Chief Executive

The Chief Executive of Visitron, Stanley Greenstock, criticises Hamilton's interpretation of the market situation.

GREENSTOCK: *Mr Hamilton. I want to take you up on* the points you made about prices. You linked our lower market shares directly to our higher prices. *Looking at it from another point of view,* isn't it possible that we failed to demonstrate our superior quality to the market?

HAMILTON: Er . . . *if I understand you correctly . . . you're saying that* with more advertising and promotion of our products Visitron could have maintained its prices *and* its market shares . . .

GREENSTOCK: We undoubtedly have a quality edge in all three sectors.

HAMILTON: But as I said during my presentation Mr Greenstock, if there is a choice between quality and price the market is more and more choosing price.

GREENSTOCK: *You still haven't answered my question* Mr Hamilton. With a bigger marketing effort . . . especially in the area of corporate advertising . . . we might have kept our prices with little or no loss of market share.

HAMILTON: *With all due respect* Mr Greenstock, Visitron is not a new company in this field. Customers know that Visitron means quality. I don't think that corporate advertising would make any difference to the present situation. *The fact is that* the market now assumes a minimum quality from all the manufacturers and it makes its purchasing decisions accordingly . . .

GREENSTOCK: *What exactly do you mean by that?*

HAMILTON: *I mean that* the market has discounted the extra quality we offer. The user needs scans as temporary references so that they can make quick medical or engineering decisions. They don't need portrait pictures for that.

GREENSTOCK: Perhaps we should be selling X-rays Mr Hamilton?

HAMILTON: We're selling the right products Mr Greenstock. But we're trying to sell them at the wrong prices.

Questions and answers: language analysis

The gambits and phrases in italics above are explained below in terms of their communicative functions in the dialogue.

The black arrows represent the people asking the questions and the white arrows the people replying to them.

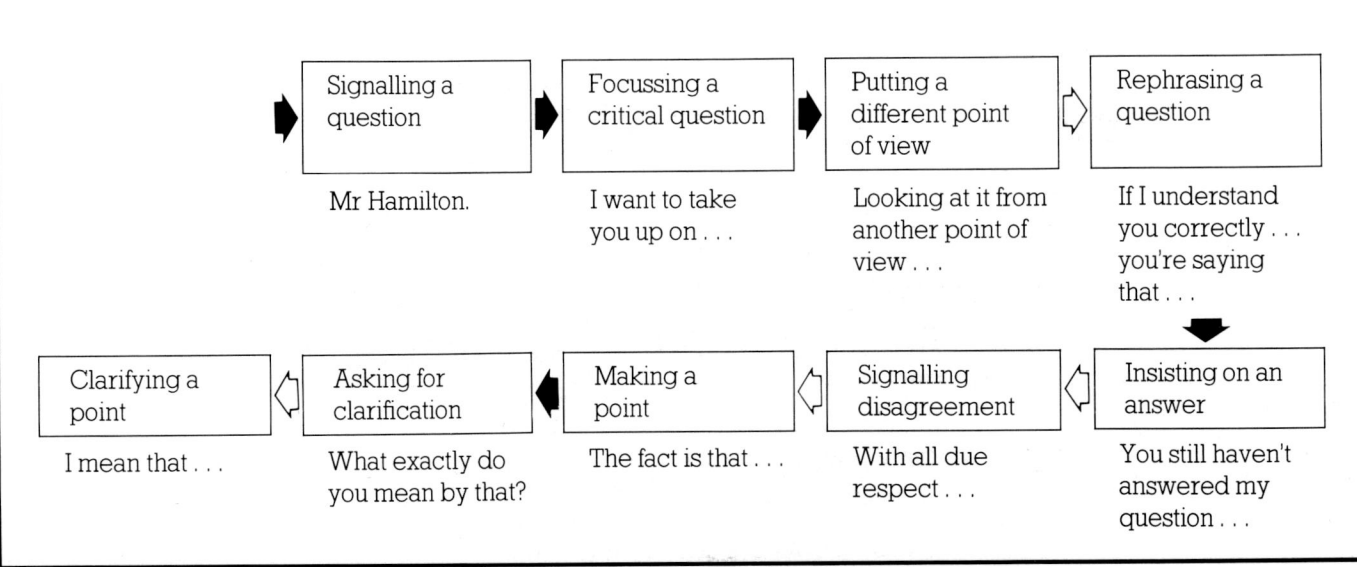

Signalling a question	Focussing a critical question	Putting a different point of view	Rephrasing a question
Mr Hamilton.	I want to take you up on . . .	Looking at it from another point of view . . .	If I understand you correctly . . . you're saying that . . .

Clarifying a point	Asking for clarification	Making a point	Signalling disagreement	Insisting on an answer
I mean that . . .	What exactly do you mean by that?	The fact is that . . .	With all due respect . . .	You still haven't answered my question . . .

UNIT 6
Describing markets

Preview

Language points

Hamilton describes the present market situation, compares Visitron's market shares with its competitors' and looks ahead.

Describing markets

... dominant positions ...
... satisfactory
20 per cent penetration ...

Forecasting

... our current forecasts show ...
Our expectations are ...

Comparing and contrasting

... Visitron's share is 16 per cent lower than in 1981 whereas Kamakura's is 1 per cent lower ...

Presentation points and preview questions

Hamilton continues to build his argument step by step. In the last section he identified price as the key factor in the market's purchasing decisions. He now shows how neglect of the price factor has damaged Visitron's market share. He uses two diagrams as illustrations. One diagram shows changes in sector shares and the other shows changes in overall market shares.

Which is the fastest growing sector of the market?

MARKET GROWTH AND SHARES BY SECTOR 1981-1991 (PROJECTED)

Small Unit sector
1981 £94m 1986 £207m 1991 £350m

Medium Unit sector
1981 £150m 1986 £152m 1991 £194m

Large Unit sector
1981 £131m 1986 £147m 1991 £154m

- Kamakura
- Visitron
- Hyperscan

What is expected to happen to Visitron's share of the Small Unit sector?

What's the picture in the Large Unit sector?

How much larger is Hyperscan's overall share this year compared with '81?

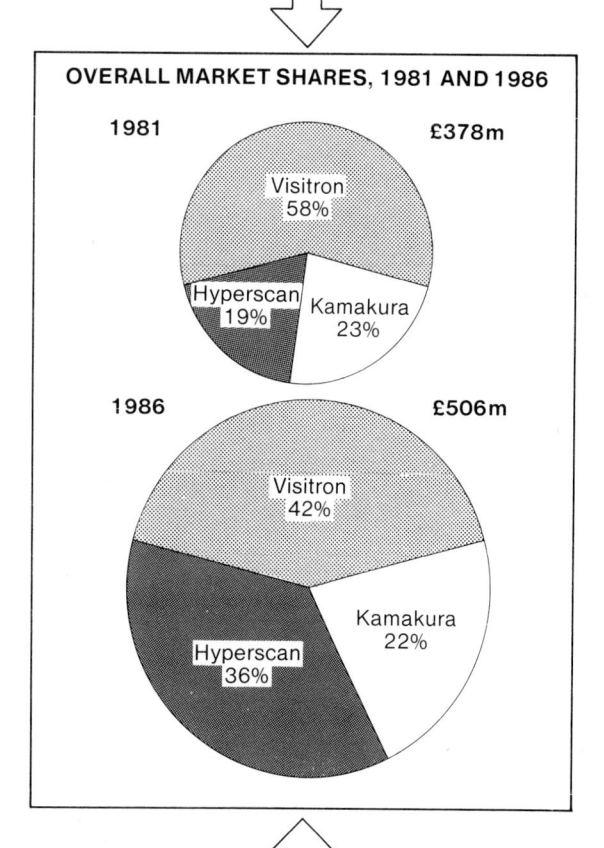

OVERALL MARKET SHARES, 1981 AND 1986

1981 — £378m
- Visitron 58%
- Hyperscan 19%
- Kamakura 23%

1986 — £506m
- Visitron 42%
- Hyperscan 36%
- Kamakura 22%

What has happened to Visitron's overall share over this period?

Summary and quick reference

6.1 Describing markets

Hyperscan	entered went into penetrated won a share of took a slice of	the Large Unit sector in 1986.
Visitron	had a dominant position in	the Large Unit sector.
Some people in Visitron want to	pull out of withdraw from come out of	the Small Unit sector.
Hyperscan's Visitron's	share of the Small Unit sector	increased . . . fell . . . expanded . . . contracted . . . grew . . . shrank . . .

6.2 Forecasting

Our forecasts show We forecast We expect We predict We anticipate	that that that that that	inflation will fall next year.
We forecast We expect We predict We anticipate	a fall in inflation next year.	
We expect	inflation to fall next year.	

6.3 Comparing and contrasting

Hyperscan's prices are	low. lower than Visitron's. the lowest.	
Visitron's machines are	expensive. more expensive than Hyperscan's. the most expensive.	
Visitron's machines are Kamakura's machines are Hyperscan's machines are	expensive less expensive than Visitron's. the least expensive.	
Visitron's market share has been falling	while whereas	Hyperscan's has been rising rapidly.

6.1 Examples from the video

Visitron *had 80%* of the Large Unit sector in 1981. *This shrank to 71%* by 1986.

Kamakura's share hovered around 20% over this period.

Hyperscan *entered this sector in 1986* and immediately *took a 9% slice.*

Model questions: asking about markets

What's your market share at the moment?
What was your market share in 1980?
Who is the market leader?
When did you enter this sector of the market?
How much has the market expanded this year?
What's the total value of the market?
Why did you pull out of this sector of the market?

6.2 Examples from the video

We expect the value of this sector to rise to £350m by 1991.

We anticipate a slight fall in Kamakura's share.

We forecast a fall in Visitron's share to 6%.

Model questions: asking about forecasts

What's your forecast for the consumer sector?
What do you expect to happen in the export market?
How do you see the future in the domestic market?
What's going to happen in the industrial sector?
What do you think will happen in the Japanese market?

6.3 Examples from the video

The UK has *much lower* petrol prices than Japan.

Petrol is most *expensive* in Japan.

Petrol *is least expensive* in the UK.

The price of petrol *is lower* in France *than* in Japan.

Model questions: asking for and about comparisons

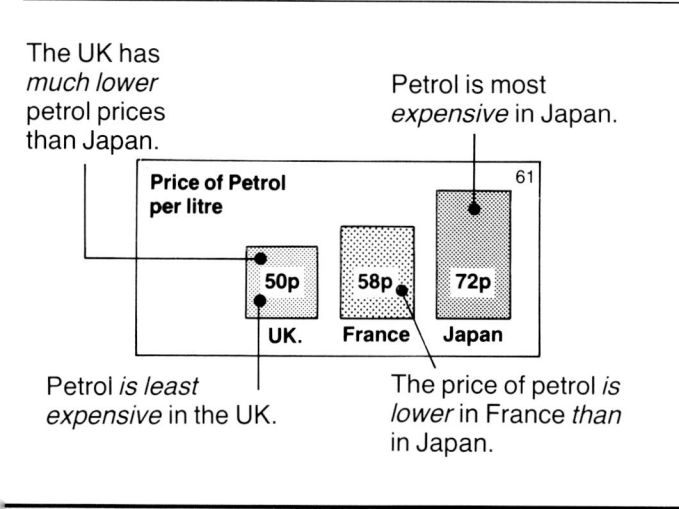

How have you compared these products?
On what basis have you made these comparisons?
Have you got any comparative figures for the domestic market?
How does product X compare with product Y?
How do competitor X's prices compare with ours?

Follow-up

Here is an example of the questions and answers which might follow this section of the presentation.

More questions from the Sales and Marketing Director

Sheila Appleton, the Sales and Marketing Director, makes a point about Visitron's market shares and questions Hamilton about the danger of losing the government contracts.

APPLETON: *I'd like to take issue with you* on one point, Mr Hamilton. *You mentioned* the erosion of our dominant positions in the Large and Medium Unit sectors. *Could I just point out that* we still have those dominant positions and that in my view a loss of 4.5 per cent of the Medium Unit sector over five years is a very good performance in such a competitive market.

HAMILTON: *I take your point* as far as the Medium Unit sector is concerned. *However*, in the Large Unit sector you have dropped nine per cent of your share in six months, which, if I may say so, is hardly satisfactory . . .

APPLETON: Yes, but . . .

HAMILTON: *Sorry* Mrs Appleton . . . *Could I just finish?* *I'd also like to remind you of* our general conclusion . . . that, even with these dominant market shares, Visitron is no longer able to make a good enough return on these products.

APPLETON: *Don't misunderstand me*, Mr Hamilton. *I agree with* your main conclusions. I just want to make sure we don't overreact. Once we concede lower prices, we will find it very hard to recapture that premium position.

HAMILTON: *I understand your concern. It's our view, however*, that Visitron no longer has a choice.

APPLETON: *OK*, Mr Hamilton. *We can discuss this later. There's just one further question*. How serious is your concern about the loss of government contracts?

HAMILTON: Very serious. The government has recently published new guidelines for state industries, and with the tenders for the new generation equipment due in 1988, I think we can expect a much harder fight next time.

APPLETON: But we are still the only British manufacturer.

HAMILTON: Yes, Mrs Appleton. And 'value for money' is still the Government's major slogan.

Questions and answers: language analysis

The gambits and phrases in italics above are explained below in terms of their communicative functions in the dialogue.

The black arrows represent the people asking the questions and the white arrows the people replying to them.

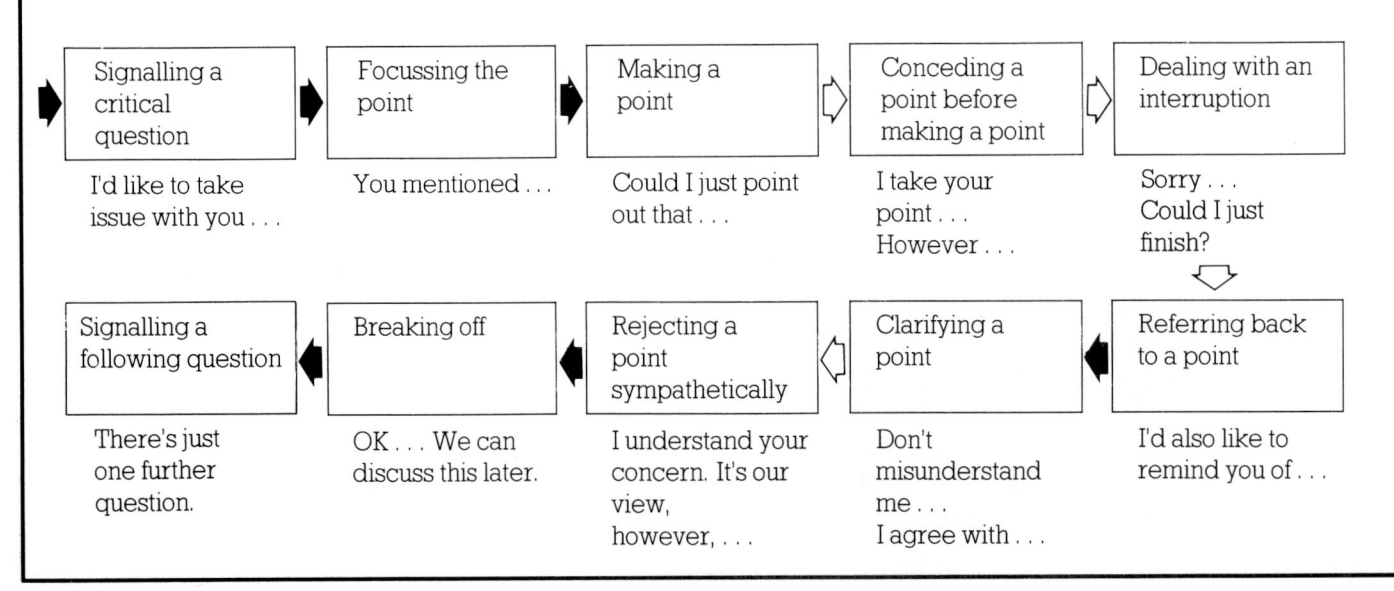

Signalling a critical question	Focussing the point	Making a point	Conceding a point before making a point	Dealing with an interruption
I'd like to take issue with you . . .	You mentioned . . .	Could I just point out that . . .	I take your point . . . However . . .	Sorry . . . Could I just finish?

Signalling a following question	Breaking off	Rejecting a point sympathetically	Clarifying a point	Referring back to a point
There's just one further question.	OK . . . We can discuss this later.	I understand your concern. It's our view, however, . . .	Don't misunderstand me . . . I agree with . . .	I'd also like to remind you of . . .

UNIT 7
Describing the financial situation

Preview

Language points

Hamilton moves on to look at the profit and loss situation in each of Visitron's three divisions.

Moving on and looking back	*Referring*	*Talking about profit and loss*
Let's now move on to . . . This brings me to . . .	. . . with respect to . . . With reference to . . .	Our trading profits come from . . .

Presentation points and preview questions

Hamilton indicates that he has completed his review of the market situation and is now ready to go on to questions of finance. The profitability of each of Visitron's three divisions is displayed on a bar chart where it is compared with the proportion of sales and capital employed in those divisions. Hamilton identifies the main problem areas and points to the major causes of those problems.

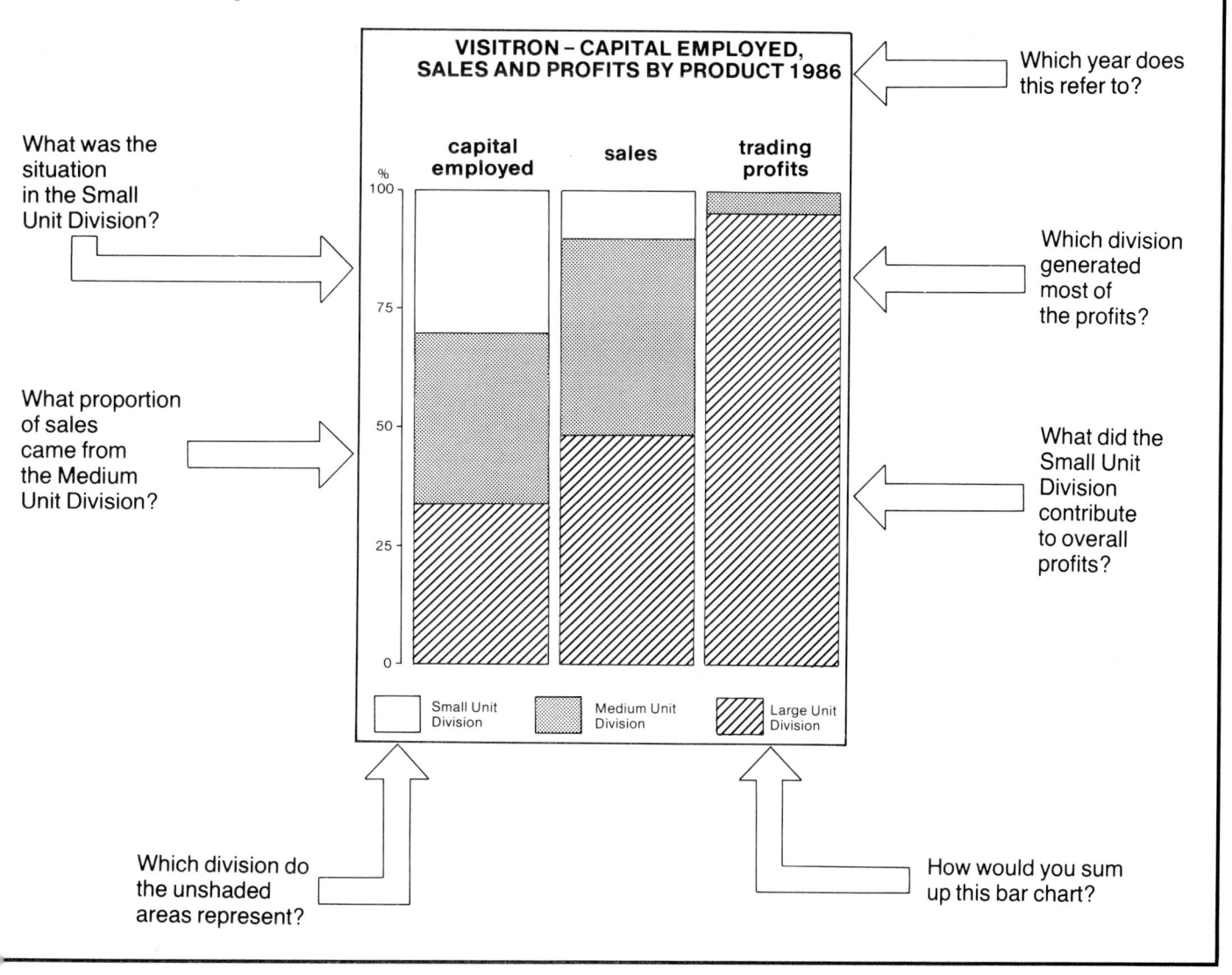

VISITRON – CAPITAL EMPLOYED, SALES AND PROFITS BY PRODUCT 1986

- Which year does this refer to?
- What was the situation in the Small Unit Division?
- Which division generated most of the profits?
- What proportion of sales came from the Medium Unit Division?
- What did the Small Unit Division contribute to overall profits?
- Which division do the unshaded areas represent?
- How would you sum up this bar chart?

Legend: Small Unit Division, Medium Unit Division, Large Unit Division

25

Summary and quick reference

7.1 Moving on and looking back

Let's now move on to I now want to go on to I'd now like to go on to This brings me to	the financial aspects of the problem.
The losses were due to the strike	but I shall come to this later.
Let's look back for a moment at Let's go back to	my first diagram.
As I said before	the situation is serious.

7.2 Referring

With respect to With reference to From the point of view of In terms of With regard to	sales,	the situation is improving.

As far as	profit output	is concerned	the situation has improved.
	sales jobs	are concerned	

7.3 Discussing profit and loss

Visitron	made a profit	of just under £1m in 1986.
The Small Unit division	made a loss	of over £3m.
The Medium Unit division	broke even	last year.
Visitron has	very high	overheads. overhead costs. indirect costs. fixed charges.
Visitron must also reduce its		variable costs. direct costs. direct charges.

7.1 Examples from the video

Let's now move on to the current situation.

1. Historical review [64]
2. Current situation
3. Options
4. Recommendations
5. Conclusions

Let's look back for a moment at our options.

This brings me to the options.

Model questions: asking about presentation structure

Can we go back to your first point?
Could we return to the question of job losses?
Could we go back to your review of the historical situation?
Can we look at your options again?
Can we go on to look at your recommendations?

7.2 Examples from the video

Population is growing.

1. Population changes [67]
2. National Income
3. Inflation
4. Unemployment
5. Exports

With respect to exports, I can say things have improved.

As far as national income is concerned, the situation is serious.

Model questions: asking about reference

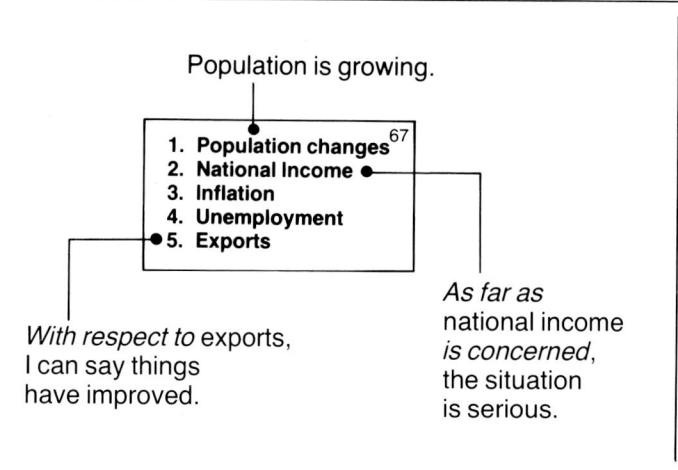

What are you referring to?
Which aspect of the problem are you talking about?
What's the situation as far as inflation is concerned?
What's happening with respect to unemployment?
What's the trend with regard to exports?

7.3 Examples from the video

— We should *break even* at 30 units.

Below 30 units *we will make a loss*.

[Graph: £ axis, Units axis, showing Break even Point, Sales, Profit, Total costs, Variable costs, Loss, 100, 30, 71]

Our *direct costs* rise quite steeply.

We will make a profit after 30 units.

Model questions: asking about profit and loss

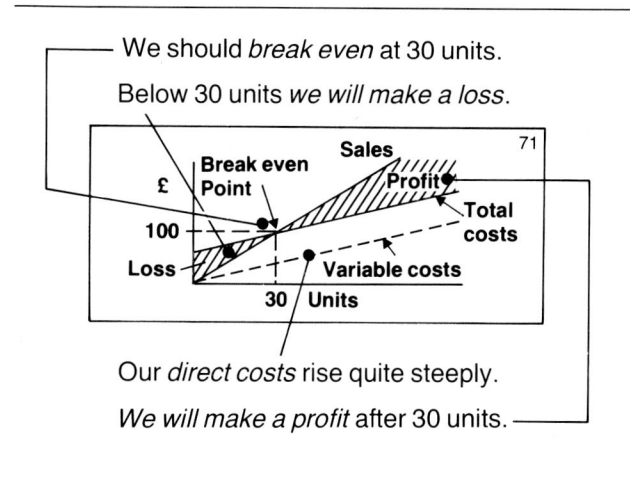

What were your profits last year?
What's our break even point?
How many units must we sell to break even?
Where did we make our main losses?
What was the loss in Division X?
How can we reduce overheads?
What is the contribution to overheads from Product Y?

Follow-up

Here is an example of the questions and answers which might follow this section of the presentation.

More questions from the Financial Director

Derek Lidburn, the Financial Director, questions Hamilton about the losses in the Small Unit division.

LIDBURN: *I have a question about* the Small Unit division losses Mr Hamilton. Er . . . *are you aware that* we introduced a rationalisation programme in that division at the end of last year?
HAMILTON: Yes I am.
LIDBURN: And are you also aware that in the last six months we have improved our contribution from the Small Unit machines by over 30 per cent?
HAMILTON: I know that a lot of progress has been made.
LIDBURN: *Then wouldn't you say* that the case for relocation has been severely weakened?
HAMILTON: Well, firstly, *as I said before*, we have not actually recommended relocation. *Be that as it may*, there are limits to the improvements you can make at the moment. *For example*, the value added per employee at Visitron is only half that per employee at Hyperscan . . . that is a very large productivity gap Mr Lidburn.
LIDBURN: *Certainly, but* a lot of that higher added value is due to Hyperscan's huge sales volume . . .
HAMILTON: *Of course . . . but* Hyperscan only achieved that huge volume by producing at low unit costs from the start. Over 1986 as a whole you failed to achieve even your present budget targets.
LIDBURN: *That leads me on to another question,* Mr Hamilton. You mentioned budget overruns. Was this a criticism of our budgeting system or the present management of that system?
HAMILTON: *To be quite frank* Mr Lidburn it was both. Your present budgeting system is based mainly on historical data. We think there is a case for zero budgeting in many areas. In other areas however we found that your present budget targets were unrealistic in the present climate . . .
LIDBURN: *Could you be more specific?*
HAMILTON: If it's OK with you Mr Lidburn, I'd prefer to leave this one to Mr Turnbull at this afternoon's session. He will be dealing with budgeting questions in full . . .

Questions and answers: language analysis

The gambits and phrases in italics above are explained below in terms of their communicative functions in the dialogue.

The black arrows represent the people asking the questions and the white arrows the people replying to them.

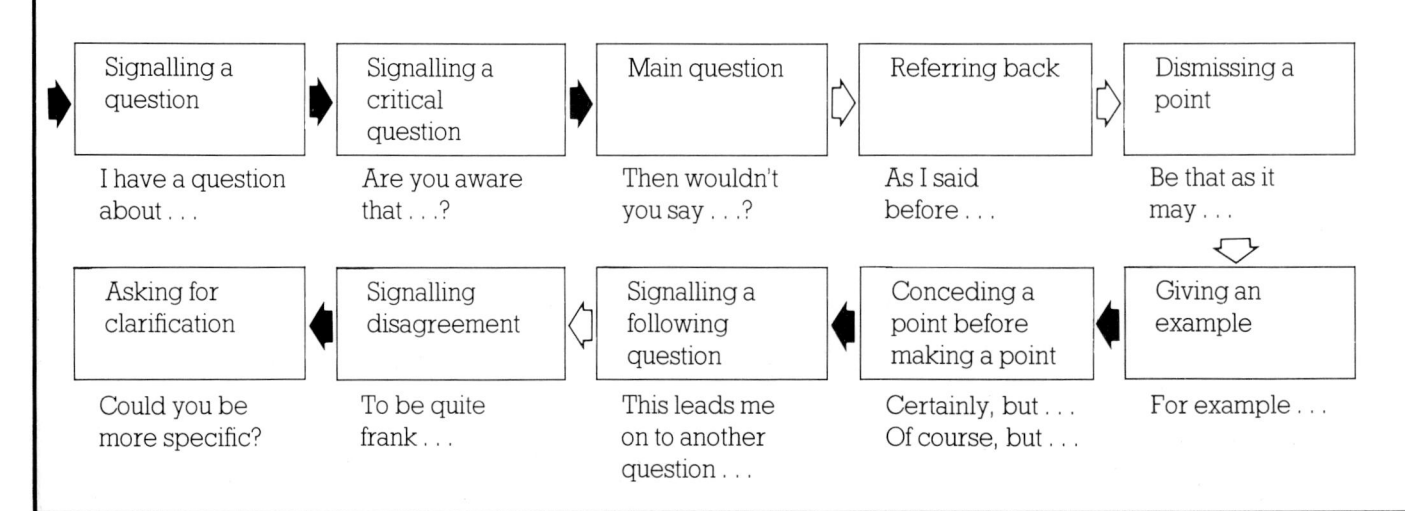

Signalling a question	Signalling a critical question	Main question	Referring back	Dismissing a point
I have a question about . . .	Are you aware that . . . ?	Then wouldn't you say . . . ?	As I said before . . .	Be that as it may . . .

Asking for clarification	Signalling disagreement	Signalling a following question	Conceding a point before making a point	Giving an example
Could you be more specific?	To be quite frank . . .	This leads me on to another question . . .	Certainly, but . . . Of course, but . . .	For example . . .

UNIT 8
Interpreting the evidence

Preview

Language points

Hamilton gives some opinions on the basis of the evidence he has presented so far. He also anticipates a later point by way of a digression.

Expressing opinions	Interpreting information	Digressing
We don't think...	Our findings show that...	Let me digress...
It is our view that...	This seems to suggest that...	I'd just like to mention in passing...

Presentation points and preview questions

Hamilton is now approaching the turning point in his presentation. He has completed his evidence and now ends that section of his presentation by summarising his case in a short, descriptive paragraph. In this paragraph he clearly identifies the major weakness in the company's strategy since 1975. He then introduces a later area of controversy by using a digression. By identifying the problem early without giving a direct opinion, he helps to soften the criticism which he will present later.

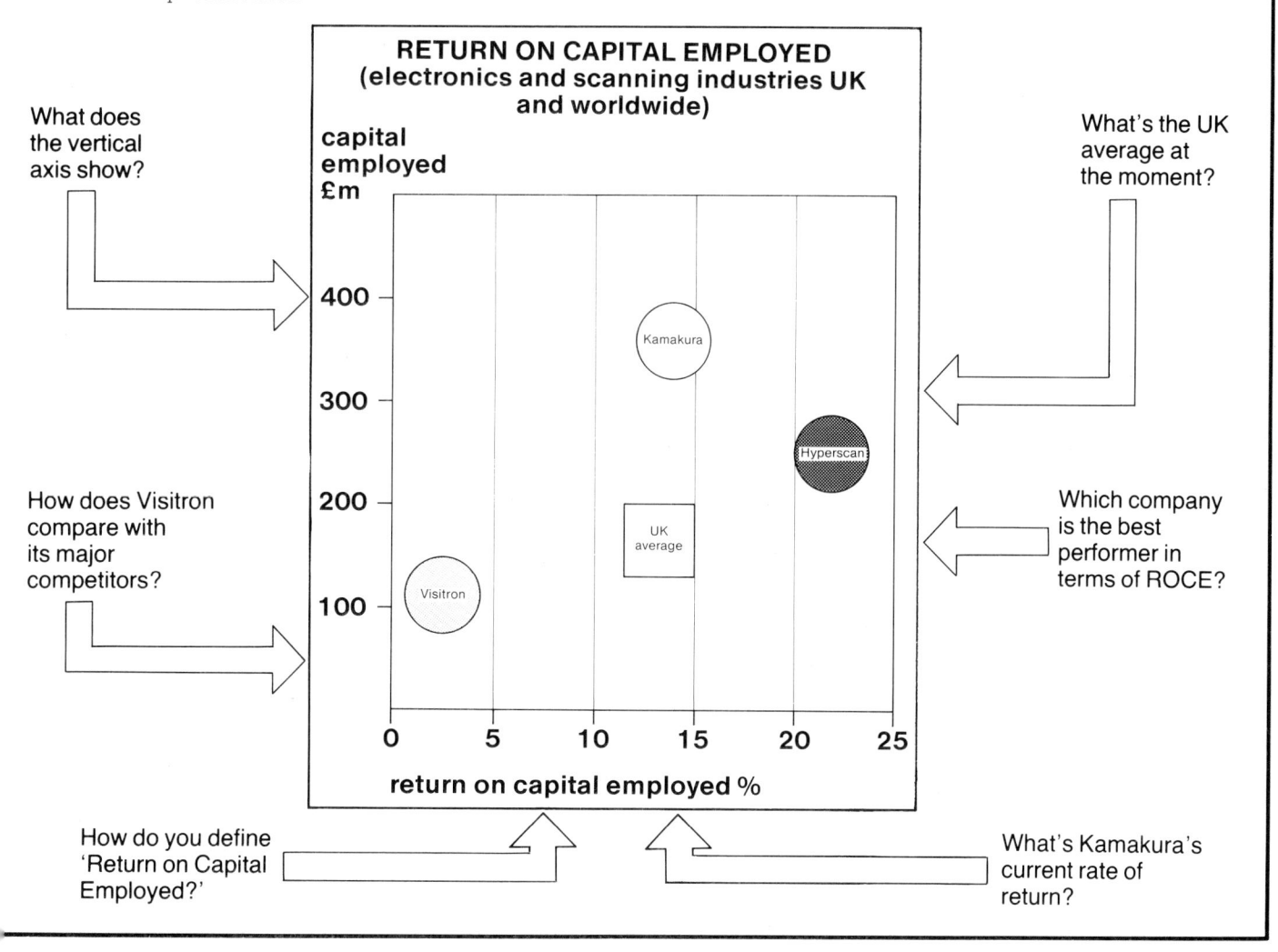

RETURN ON CAPITAL EMPLOYED
(electronics and scanning industries UK and worldwide)

- What does the vertical axis show?
- How does Visitron compare with its major competitors?
- What's the UK average at the moment?
- Which company is the best performer in terms of ROCE?
- How do you define 'Return on Capital Employed?'
- What's Kamakura's current rate of return?

Summary and quick reference

8.1 Expressing opinions

We believe	(that)	
We think	(that)	your prices are too high.
It is our view	that	
My opinion is	that	
I would say	(that)	
It seems to us	that	you should concentrate on the mass market product.
We feel	that	
We tend to feel	that	

8.2 Interpreting information

Our findings show The results show	a fall	in the rate of return on capital employed.
The figures indicate It is quite clear	that	return on capital employed has fallen.
This seems to suggest This would seem to show	that	the situation has worsened.
These figures seem to indicate This may suggest	a worsening	of the situation.

8.3 Digressing

Let me digress here I'd like to digress here	for a moment.	
I'd just like to mention in passing		that the situation in our other markets is not quite so bad.
In passing On quite another matter	could I say	
Let me get back to	my main point.	
	what I was saying.	

8.1 Examples from the video

I think that income tax is too high.

I would say the price of oil will fall.

74
1. Income Tax
2. Trade Unions
3. The United Nations
4. The price of oil

It is my view that trade unions play an important part in democratic societies.

Model questions: asking about opinions

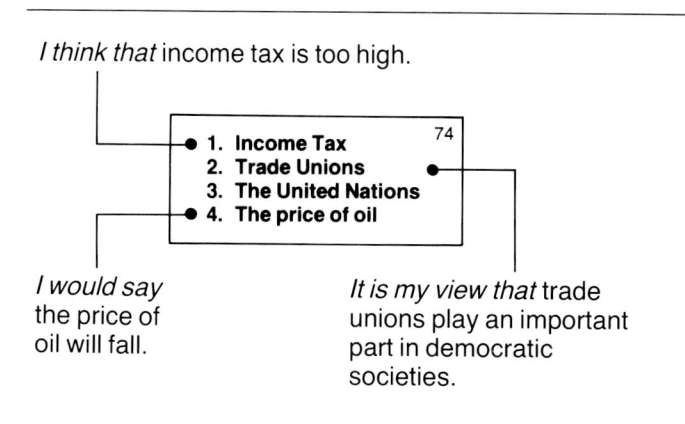

What do you think about the present rate of income tax?
What's your opinion of the new product?
What would you say is our best strategy?
Who do you feel is the best man for the job?
What's your view of the present situation?

8.2 Examples from the video

Our survey shows that comfort and price are the most important factors.

77
Price, Fuel Economy, Reliability, Comfort

The figures seem to show that fuel economy is the third most important factor.

It is quite clear that reliability is not very important in customers' decisions to buy.

Model questions: asking about interpretations

How do you justify this?
What does this survey show?
What's your evidence for this?
What's the basis for these figures?
What sample did you use for this survey?
Where did you get these figures from?

8.3 Examples from the video

80

Theme	Digression
People change to tea ↑ Health dangers ↑ Tax on coffee +5% ↑ Price of coffee +15% ↑	Your view of coffee drinking. eg. 'Personally I like/dislike . . .'

I'd like to point out that since the price of coffee has gone up by 15% and the tax has risen by 5% we must expect a fall in demand for this product. *Let me say in passing* that personally, I dislike coffee and I'm sure many people share my view. Anyway, *let me get back to my main point.* People are changing to tea.

Model questions: asking about digressions

What's the relevance of this?
What's this got to do with what I was saying?
Aren't you sidetracking a little here?
Can we keep to the point?
Could we get back to the main point?

Follow-up

Here is an example of the questions and answers which might follow this section of the presentation.

More questions from the Chief Executive

Stanley Greenstock, Chief Executive and architect of the 1975 Plan, makes some further critical remarks about Hamilton's overall analysis.

GREENSTOCK: *Can I be quite frank with you? It . . . er . . . seems to me that* you are being wise after the event. Of course it's easy, with the benefit of hindsight, to identify the weaknesses in any particular strategy. Even so, do you really believe that the launch of our first Small Unit scanner and the introduction of a new generation of our other scanners was merely . . . how did you put it . . . a corporate facelift?

HAMILTON: *Please don't get me wrong* Mr Greenstock. There were many very positive achievements in the 1975 Plan. *My point was that* it failed to tackle the underlying manufacturing problem. Yes . . . *it gave us* a technical lead and complete market coverage for the first time since 1972. *What it did not give us* however, *was* the ability to convert good products into hard sales.

GREENSTOCK: Fine words Mr Hamilton but don't forget you're talking about 1975. Things were different then.

HAMILTON: *Of course they were* . . . and *I agree* it would have been difficult then to predict the huge increases in productivity coming from our competitors in the Far East and Pacific Basin. *Nevertheless* Visitron . . . along with many other major corporations . . . failed to adapt.

GREENSTOCK: Yes I understood your general point. But *let me put another point to you*. Success in the Small Unit sector depends heavily on economies of scale. So far we do not have markets outside Europe. Perhaps then you are trying to lead us into very deep and dangerous waters when you suggest that we stay in this sector?

HAMILTON: Mm . . . *well first of all* we believe that the European market alone will provide all the necessary economies of scale. *Furthermore however*, we believe that without a strong presence in this sector you will not be able to defend your other sectors. *Most importantly though*, this is the growth area for the next ten years. It would be unwise to ignore it Mr Greenstock.

Questions and answers: language analysis

The gambits and phrases in italics above are explained below in terms of their communicative functions in the dialogue.

The black arrows represent the people asking the questions and the white arrows the people replying to them.

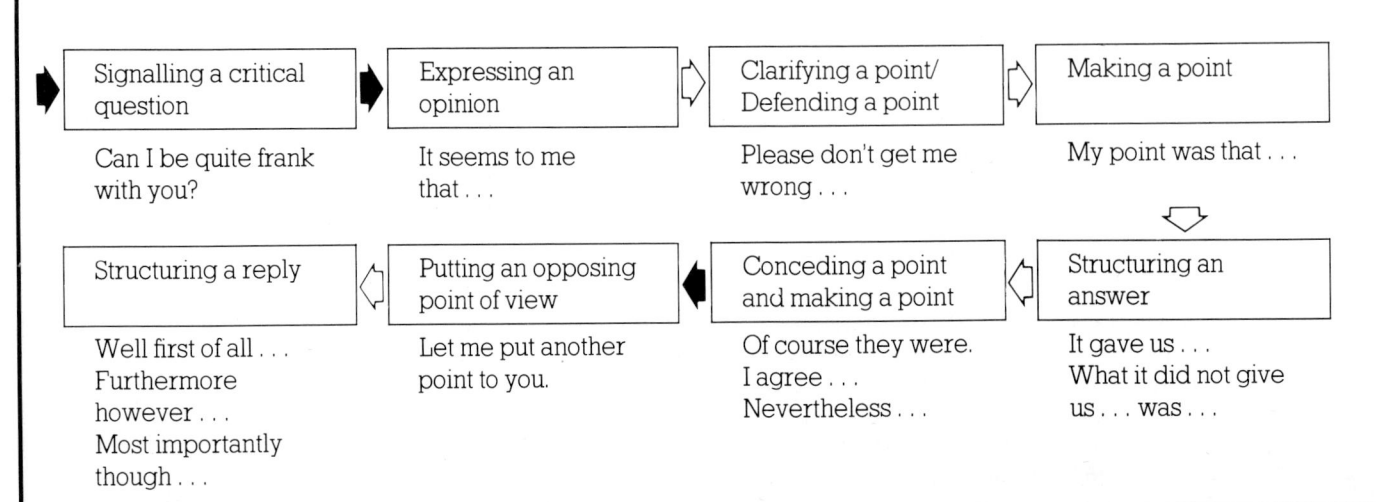

Signalling a critical question	Expressing an opinion	Clarifying a point/ Defending a point	Making a point
Can I be quite frank with you?	It seems to me that . . .	Please don't get me wrong . . .	My point was that . . .

Structuring a reply	Putting an opposing point of view	Conceding a point and making a point	Structuring an answer
Well first of all . . . Furthermore however . . . Most importantly though . . .	Let me put another point to you.	Of course they were. I agree . . . Nevertheless . . .	It gave us . . . What it did not give us . . . was . . .

UNIT 9
Getting to the heart of the matter

Preview

Language points

Hamilton summarises his argument so far, identifies the underlying cause of the company's problems and shows the changes that must be made.

Warning	*Reinforcing a point*	*Getting to the point*
Unless we . . .	In addition to this . . .	What I'm getting at is . . .
If we don't . . .	Furthermore . . .	Let me come to the point.

Presentation points and preview questions

Hamilton has now brought his presentation to the point where he can turn to the future and prepare his audience for his recommendations. Before entering the final stages of his presentation however he summarises his main points so far and restates his main thesis in one brief paragraph. He follows this immediately with a single sentence signpost to the future.

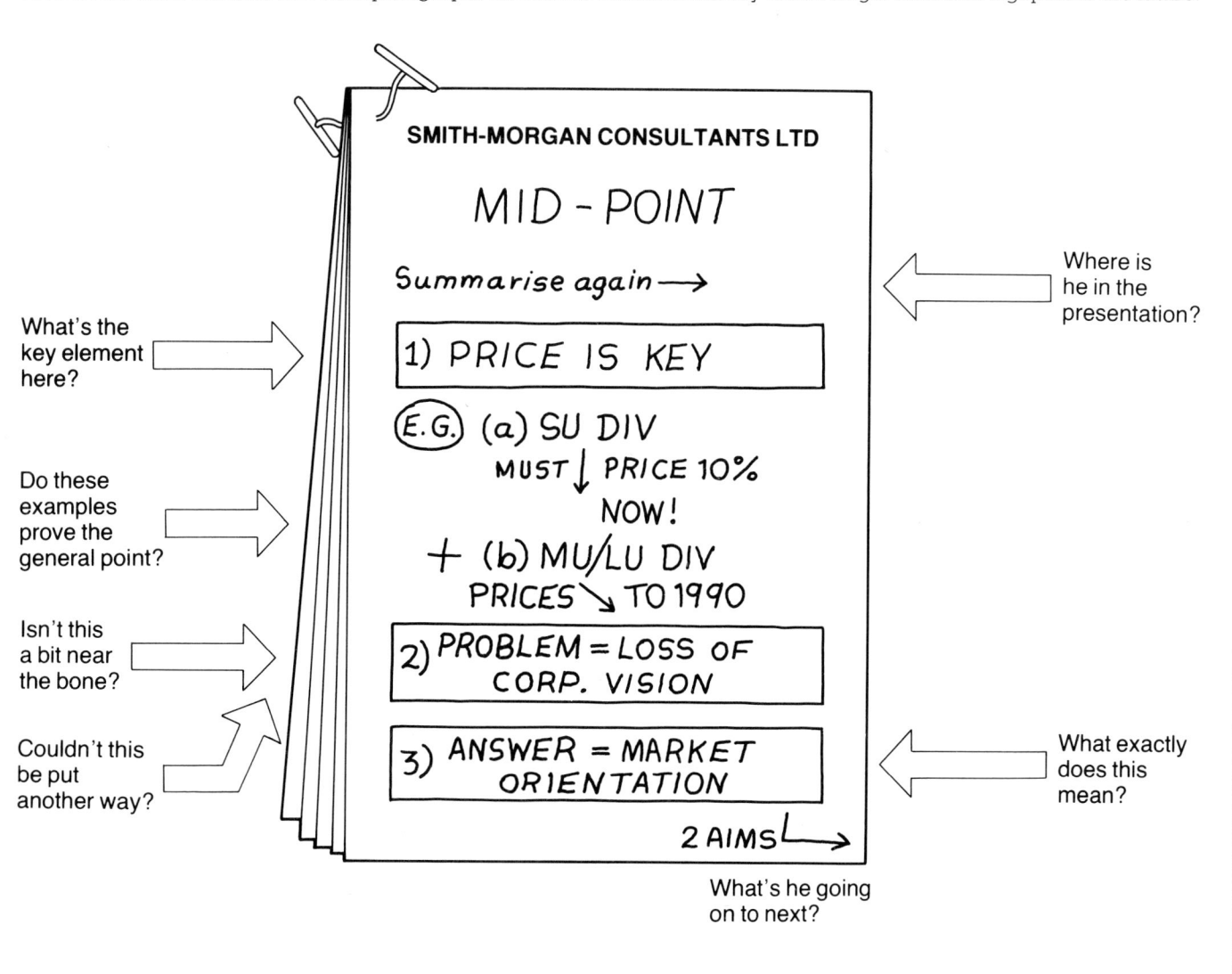

SMITH-MORGAN CONSULTANTS LTD

MID - POINT

Summarise again →

1) PRICE IS KEY

E.G. (a) SU DIV
MUST ↓ PRICE 10% NOW!
+ (b) MU/LU DIV
PRICES ↘ TO 1990

2) PROBLEM = LOSS OF CORP. VISION

3) ANSWER = MARKET ORIENTATION

2 AIMS ↳

Where is he in the presentation?

What's the key element here?

Do these examples prove the general point?

Isn't this a bit near the bone?

Couldn't this be put another way?

What exactly does this mean?

What's he going on to next?

Summary and quick reference

9.1 Warning

Unless we If we don't If Visitron does not	cut costs	profits will continue to fall.
If Visitron Provided that Visitron	cuts costs	profits will stop falling.

9.2 Reinforcing a point

In addition to this What is more Furthermore Moreover	we must also reduce our manning levels.
But most importantly But above all Most importantly however	we must become more market-oriented.

9.3 Getting to the point

What I'm getting at is The crux of the matter is My thesis is My main point is What I'm saying is	that management has failed to grasp important opportunities.
Let me come to the point.	Management has failed to grasp important opportunities.

9.1 Examples from the video

Unless we reduce prices our market share will fall.

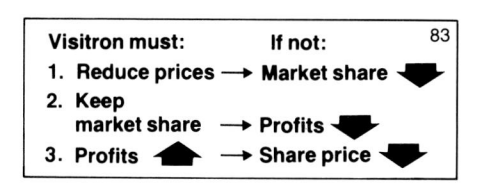

```
Visitron must:        If not:              83
1. Reduce prices  →  Market share ▼
2. Keep
   market share   →  Profits ▼
3. Profits ▲      →  Share price ▼
```

If we don't keep our market share our profits will fall.

Model questions: possible actions and their results

What will happen if we don't reduce our prices?
What will happen if we raise our prices?
How can we stop the fall in profits?
What are the dangers here?
How can we avoid this problem?

9.2 Examples from the video

Smoking is dirty. *Furthermore* it is expensive. *But most importantly* it is dangerous.

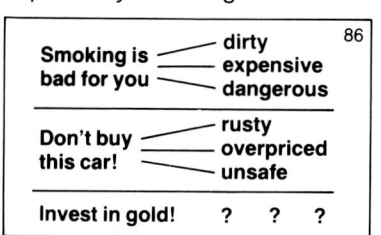

```
                    ┌ dirty           86
Smoking is  ─── expensive
bad for you         └ dangerous

                ┌ rusty
Don't buy   ─── overpriced
this car!       └ unsafe

Invest in gold!   ?  ?  ?
```

Don't buy this car. It's rusty. *What is more,* it's overpriced. *But above all* it's unsafe.

Model questions: asking about particular points

Why did you emphasise this point?
Sorry . . . why is this so important?
What's the most important factor here?
Which of these points do you consider the most important?

9.3 Examples from the video

```
1. Profitability              88
   is falling.
                    ↘ There is
2. Share price   →  a risk
   has plunged.    ↗ of takeover.
3. Assets are
   undervalued.
```

There are three main factors here. Profitability is falling, the share price has plunged and our assets are undervalued. *What I'm getting at is that* there is a real risk of a takeover.

Model questions: asking about the speaker's main message

What are you getting at?
What are you saying?
What are you trying to say?
What's the real problem here?
What's your main argument?
What's the key to all this?

Follow-up

Here is an example of the questions and answers which might follow this section of the presentation.

More questions from the Production Director

Robert Scott, the Production Director, defends the present management team's performance since 1975. Sheila Appleton supports him but Sir David Stokes takes Hamilton's side.

SCOTT: *Can I just say something in defence of* the present management team Mr Hamilton? Of course I understand that your brief was to present a critical analysis of our corporate performance... *and let me add immediately* that I'm sure most of us here would agree with your general conclusions... *I feel* however *that* your reference to a... what was it?... a loss of corporate vision, was not entirely justified.

HAMILTON: OK... *let me put my remarks into a proper perspective* Mr Scott. The 1970s were an extremly difficult period for industry. Everything changed in October 1973 and it took many years for many major corporations to detect the new business trends. In fact very few companies adapted successfully to the oil shock in the short run. Visitron was certainly not alone in this respect Mr Scott.

SCOTT: *OK. But my point was that* in many areas we did adapt successfully. You yourself pointed out that we managed to maintain our premium prices in the Large Unit sector until this year. I wouldn't call that a loss of vision. I would call that very clear thinking indeed.

HAMILTON: *I would agree with you up to a point.* Your performance in the Large Unit sector has certainly been the key to your survival so far. In other areas however you were not so successful. I'm thinking mainly of the failure to exploit the growth of the Small Unit sector and the inability to react quickly to competitive moves...

SCOTT: *You're referring to* the Large Unit sector again?

HAMILTON: That's one example.

APPLETON: *You may be interested to know that* our share in that sector has picked up since we reduced our prices there...

SIR DAVID: OK, Sheila. But *I think that only proves* Richard's *point.* We have only stabilised our market share by reducing our unit contribution.

HAMILTON: I'm afraid that's right. You are now defending your market positions by eating deep into your margins. And in the long run ladies and gentlemen, that's a recipe for corporate disaster.

Questions and answers: language analysis

The gambits and phrases in italics above are explained below in terms of their communicative functions in the dialogue.

The black arrows represent the people asking the questions and the white arrows the people replying to them.

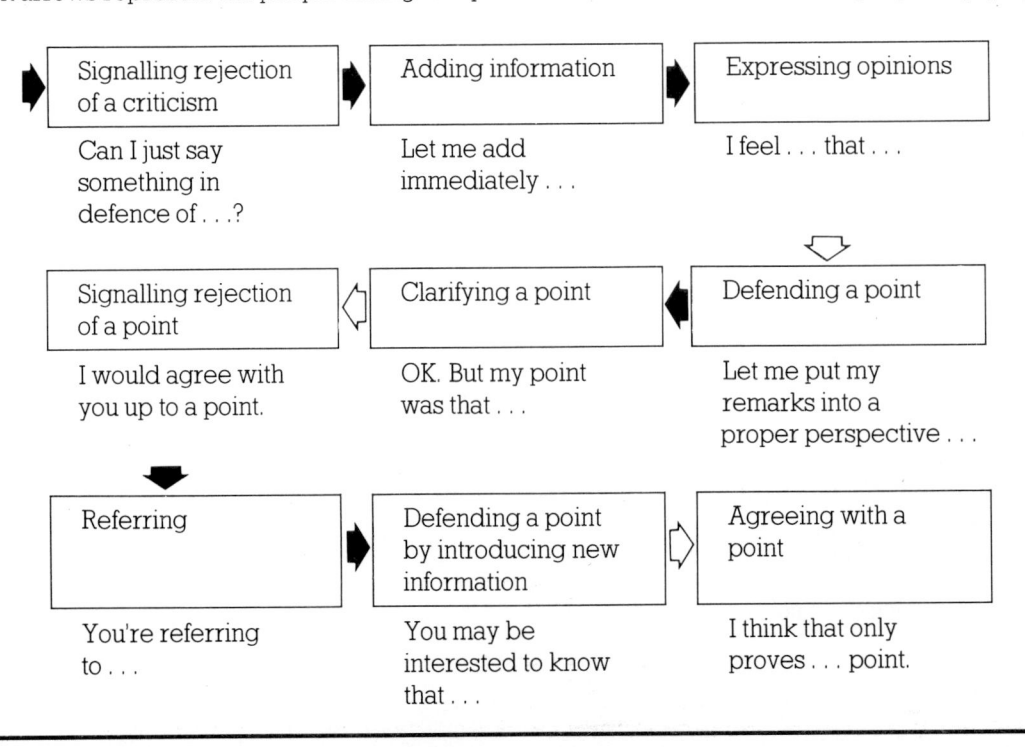

Signalling rejection of a criticism	Adding information	Expressing opinions
Can I just say something in defence of...?	Let me add immediately...	I feel... that...

Signalling rejection of a point	Clarifying a point	Defending a point
I would agree with you up to a point.	OK. But my point was that...	Let me put my remarks into a proper perspective...

Referring	Defending a point by introducing new information	Agreeing with a point
You're referring to...	You may be interested to know that...	I think that only proves... point.

UNIT 10
Turning to the future

Preview

Language points

Hamilton outlines the types of strategies needed in the future and presents targets.

Using rhetorical questions	Disagreeing	Presenting targets
The obvious question is . . .	We disagree . . .	Our major long-term target . . .
It is a question of whether . . .	We have some reservations . . .	It is vital that we . . .

Presentation points and preview questions

Hamilton now sets the scene for the final stage of his presentation. He begins by identifying the dilemma facing the company and the kinds of strategies that will be needed to solve it. He then presents a series of corporate targets.

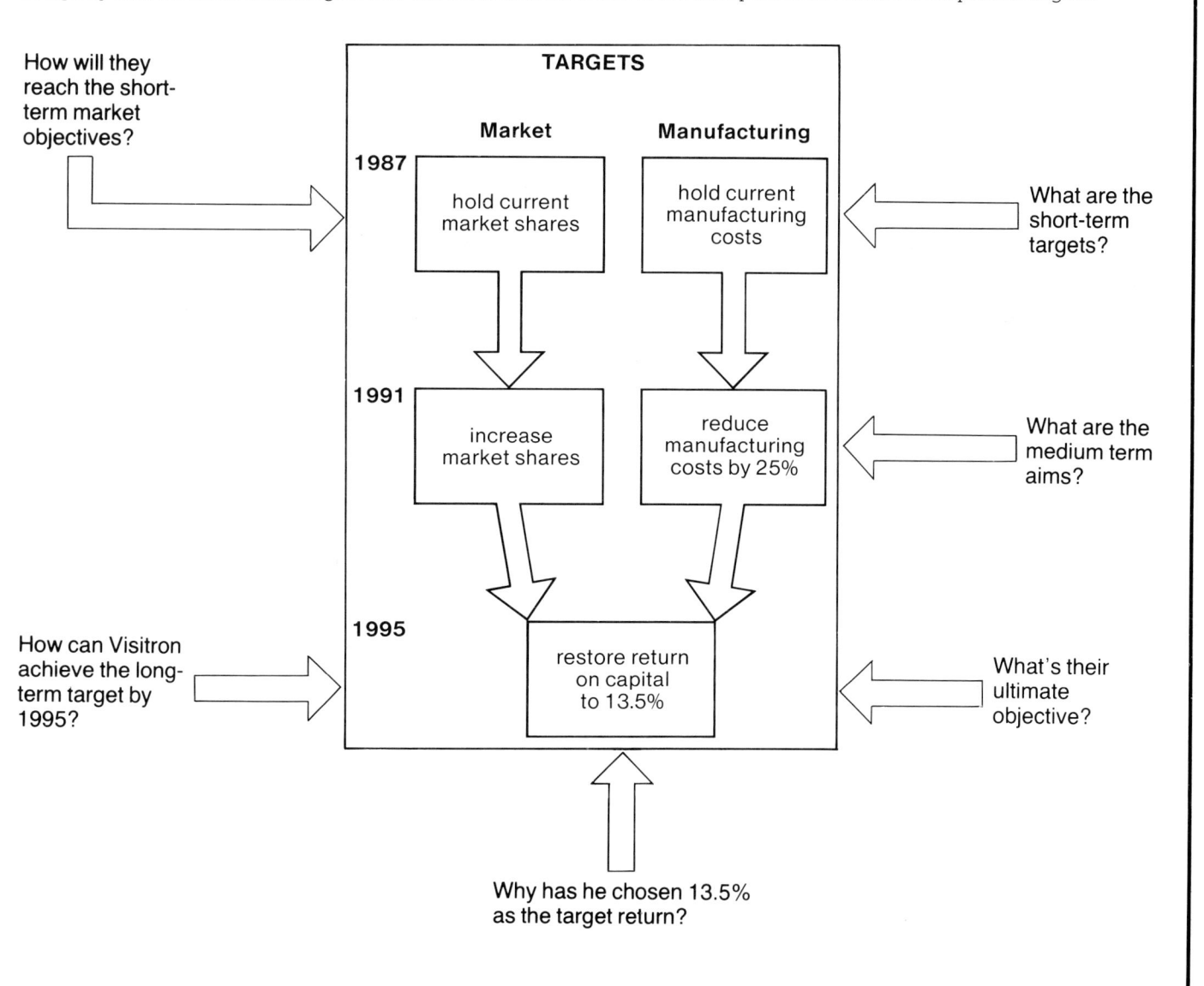

TARGETS

How will they reach the short-term market objectives? →

1987: hold current market shares | hold current manufacturing costs ← What are the short-term targets?

1991: increase market shares | reduce manufacturing costs by 25% ← What are the medium term aims?

How can Visitron achieve the long-term target by 1995? →

1995: restore return on capital to 13.5% ← What's their ultimate objective?

↑ Why has he chosen 13.5% as the target return?

Summary and quick reference

10.1 Using rhetorical questions

The obvious question is	can we	achieve these targets by 1995?
It is a question of whether The question is whether	we can	
So	who was responsible? what should we do? how much would it cost? where did we go wrong?	

10.2 Disagreeing

We disagree We cannot agree I'm afraid we disagree Unfortunately we cannot agree	with	you on this point.
We have taken careful note of your views We see your point	but	we are inclined to be more optimistic than you.
We have some reservations We are not sure	about	your first recommendation.

10.3 Presenting targets

Our major long-term target can be stated quite simply.		We must raise our return on capital.
The main target The main aim Our main objective Our first priority	must be is should be	to raise our return on capital.
It is vital It is absolutely essential	that	we raise our return on capital.
We must		raise our return on capital.

10.1 Examples from the video

It is a question of whether we should locate the factory at A or at B.

```
                                              92
    ●  a. Location A or B?
       b. Cost of construction?
       c. Personnel needed?
    ●  d. Project Leader?
       e. Pay-off period?
```

The next obvious question is who should be the project leader?

Model questions: asking about points raised by rhetorical questions

Couldn't your question be put another way?
Is that really the right question to ask?
Aren't you seeing it in rather black and white terms?

10.2 Examples from the video

I see your point about the safety aspects of nuclear power *but* many more lives have been lost in the coal industry since 1960.

```
                                              95
    The best future energy source is
 ●  A: Nuclear power.     B: Coal.

    The future of industry depends on
    A: More skilled workers.     B: Robots. ●
```

I cannot agree with you that robots will completely take over from skilled workers.

Model questions: asking about disagreements

Why exactly do you disagree with these proposals?
What are your reservations?
What's your alternative then?
What would you suggest then?
Can you be more precise about why you disagree?
How would you go about it then?

10.3 Examples from the video

Our major target should be to restore our return on capital to 13.5%.

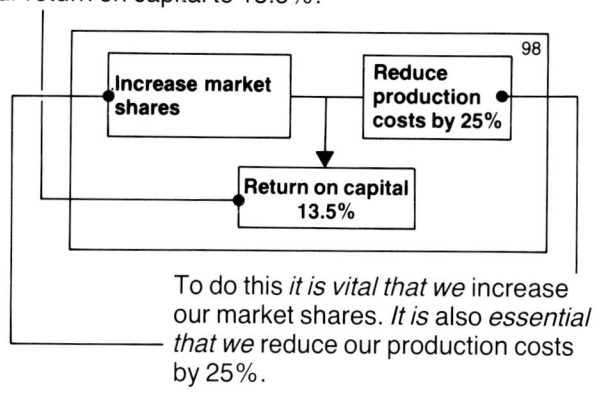

```
                                              98
   ┌─────────────┐      ┌──────────────┐
   │Increase     │      │Reduce        │
   │market       │      │production    │●
   │shares       │      │costs by 25%  │
   └─────────────┘      └──────────────┘
           │                    │
           ▼                    │
        ┌──────────────────┐    │
        │Return on capital │◄───┘
        │      13.5%       │
        └──────────────────┘
```

To do this *it is vital that we* increase our market shares. *It is* also *essential that we* reduce our production costs by 25%.

Model questions: asking about targets

What are your targets?
What should the targets be?
Are these targets realistic?
What's your primary objective?
What are your secondary aims?
How can we achieve these targets?
Why is this so vital?
Is this really essential?

Follow-up

Here is an example of the questions and answers which might follow this section of the presentation.

Questions from the Chairman

The Chairman of Visitron, Sir David Stokes, questions Hamilton about the proposed corporate targets.

SIR DAVID: *Richard... I wonder if we could go on to* the corporate targets which you proposed? *My question is whether* these targets go far enough?

HAMILTON: *In what sense* Sir David?

SIR DAVID: Well, you proposed that we reduce our costs by 25 per cent by 1991 in order to match our competitors' rapid increases in productivity in the last five years. *Supposing* they achieve similar increases in the next five years? Will a 25 per cent cost reduction be enough?

HAMILTON: *It's a good question* and, of course, we can never be absolutely certain about the future. However, we expect productivity gains to level out until the mid-1990s both in the US and the Pacific Basin...

SIR DAVID: Is that a realistic expectation? After all they have taken us by surprise several times since 1972.

HAMILTON: We think it's realistic in the present circumstances. In the past five years our competitors have invested a lot of cash in new factories and plant. To get a good return on that investment they will want a good life from that plant. This means that they will not replace it until the mid-1990s at the earliest and so there will not be any major increases in productivity until then...

SIR DAVID: Mm...

HAMILTON: *I should also add that* we have seen a 10 per cent rise in Pacific Basin wage costs since 1984. Their low labour cost advantage will not last for ever.

SIR DAVID: Won't that weaken your case for relocation?

HAMILTON: It's certainly something we must watch very carefully.

SIR DAVID: OK. *One last question* Richard. *What about* new competitors?

HAMILTON: We think it's very unlikely. The entry costs to this industry are now far too high.

SIR DAVID: What, no more surprises Richard?

HAMILTON: *Not exactly* Sir David. The surprises will be in product development. Not new competitors.

Questions and answers: language analysis

The gambits and phrases in italics above are explained below in terms of their communicative functions in the dialogue.

The black arrows represent the people asking the questions and the white arrows the people replying to them.

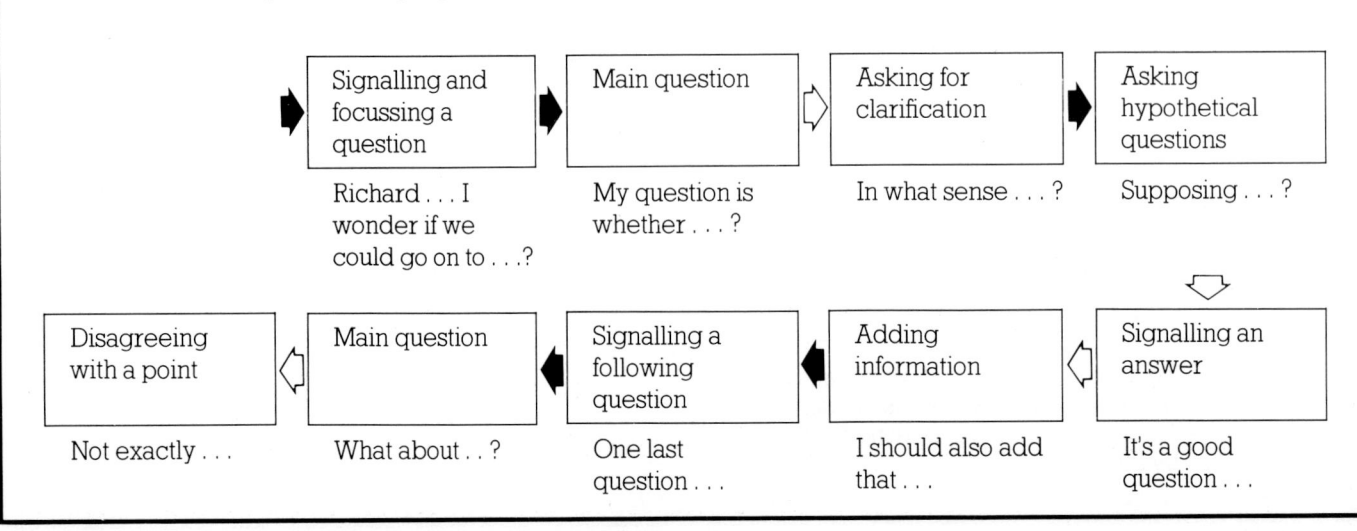

Signalling and focussing a question	Main question	Asking for clarification	Asking hypothetical questions
Richard... I wonder if we could go on to...?	My question is whether...?	In what sense...?	Supposing...?

Disagreeing with a point	Main question	Signalling a following question	Adding information	Signalling an answer
Not exactly...	What about..?	One last question...	I should also add that...	It's a good question...

UNIT 11
Presenting options – 1

Preview

Language points

Hamilton now introduces the options open to Visitron and discusses the first option in some detail.

Expressing hypothesis

In Option A we would pull out of . . .
What would happen if . . .

Developing the argument – 1

On the other hand . . .
However . . .
Furthermore . . .
Therefore . . .

Presenting calculations

We therefore estimate . . .
Our figures show . . .

Presentation points and preview questions

Hamilton now enters the final stage of his presentation. Since this is the climax of the session he prepares the way for his recommendations very carefully. First he presents a visual and analytical framework within which the options open to the company can be compared. Then he puts the first option into that framework. Once again his key statements are reinforced visually by bold and well designed diagrams.

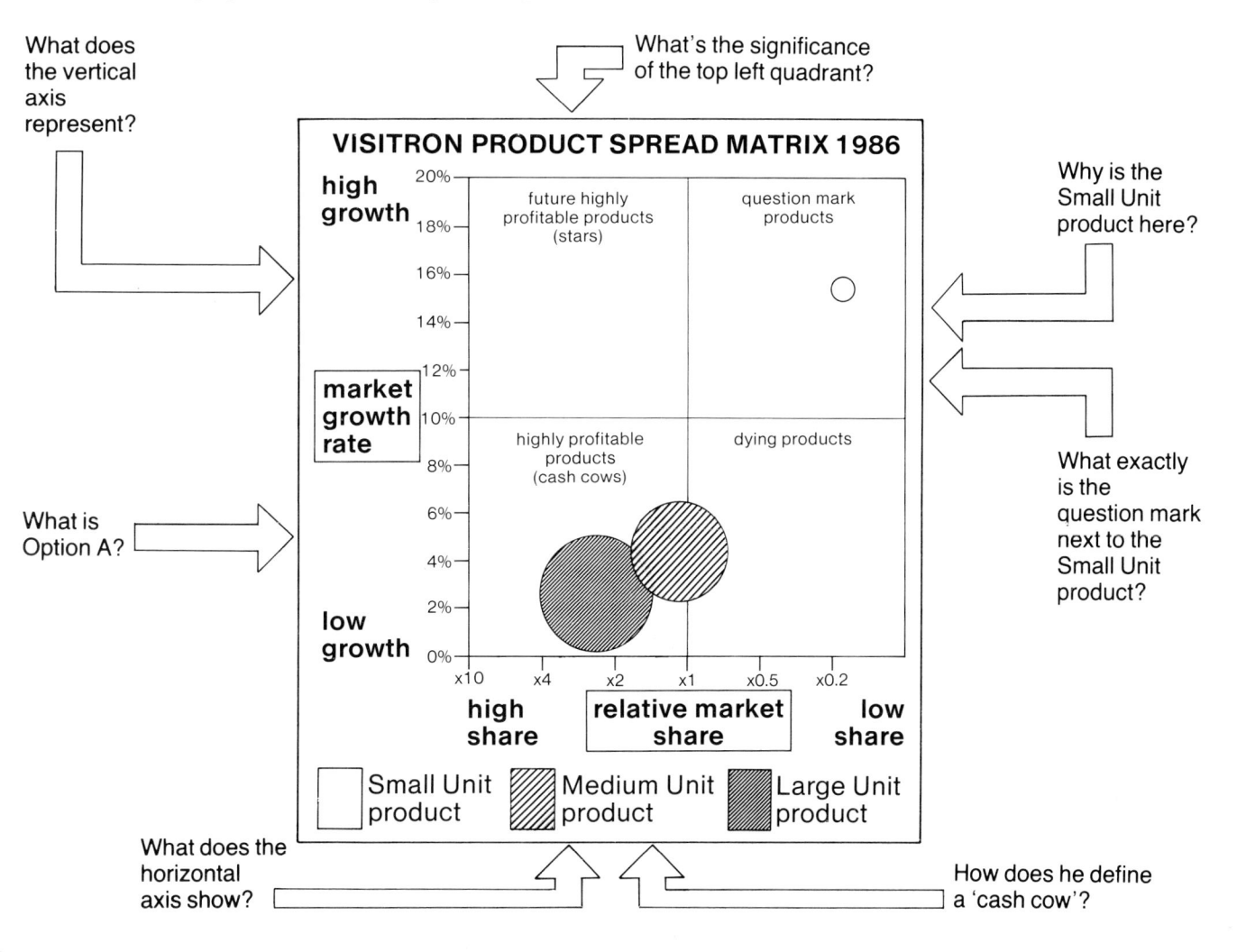

What does the vertical axis represent?

What's the significance of the top left quadrant?

VISITRON PRODUCT SPREAD MATRIX 1986

high growth — 20%, 18%, 16%, 14%
- future highly profitable products (stars)
- question mark products

market growth rate — 12%, 10%, 8%
- highly profitable products (cash cows)
- dying products

low growth — 6%, 4%, 2%, 0%

horizontal axis: x10, x4, x2, x1, x0.5, x0.2
high share — relative market share — low share

Small Unit product | Medium Unit product | Large Unit product

What is Option A?

Why is the Small Unit product here?

What exactly is the question mark next to the Small Unit product?

What does the horizontal axis show?

How does he define a 'cash cow'?

41

Summary and quick reference

11.1 Expressing hypothesis

In Option A we would pull out of this sector altogether.

If we *chose* If we *decided* upon If we *selected*	Option A	we *would save* £4m per annum.
What *would happen* What *would be* the result		if *we chose* Option A?
Suppose we *chose* Option A?		If *we chose* Option A we *would save* £4m per annum.

11.2 Developing the argument – 1

Option A would save £4m immediately.

However But On the other hand	it would also involve certain hidden costs.
Firstly	20 per cent of our customers are upgraded from our Small machines.
In addition Furthermore On top of this	there is a large contribution to overheads from these machines.
And so Therefore	the true saving from Option A would be less than £4m.

11.3 Presenting calculations

We estimate Our figures show Our sums show We calculate Our estimates indicate Our calculations show	that	our ratio of trading profit to turnover is down to 5 per cent.

11.1 Examples from the video

If someone discovered a substitute for oil, the price of oil *would fall*.

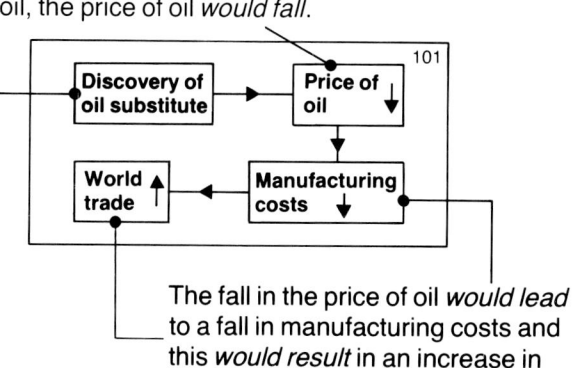

```
┌─────────────┐    ┌──────────┐
│ Discovery of│───▶│ Price of │↓
│oil substitute│    │   oil    │
└─────────────┘    └──────────┘
       ▲                │
       │                ▼
┌─────────┐        ┌──────────────┐
│ World ▲ │◀───────│Manufacturing │
│ trade   │        │ costs      ↓ │
└─────────┘        └──────────────┘
```

The fall in the price of oil *would lead* to a fall in manufacturing costs and this *would result* in an increase in world trade.

Model questions: asking about hypothesis

What would happen if we raised our prices by 5 per cent?
What would be the result of a 5 per cent price cut?
How much would our market share rise if we cut prices?
Why would Option A not be the best solution?
What would we do if that happened?

11.2 Examples from the video

1. Last year's results good. Units sold up 10%.
2. To do this, we dropped price 15%.
3. Free gifts with each sale.
4. Last year's results not as good as they appeared.

Last year's sales were up by 10%. We achieved this *however* by dropping our price by 15%. *Furthermore* we gave away free gifts with each sale. It is clear, *therefore* that last year's results were not as good as they appeared.

Model questions: asking about a line of argument

Could you run through your argument once more?
Sorry, I didn't follow your reasoning?
Could you explain again how you reached that conclusion?
I don't see the relevance of your second point?

11.3 Examples from the video

Our figures show that the ratio of trading profit to turnover was 6.3% in 1980.

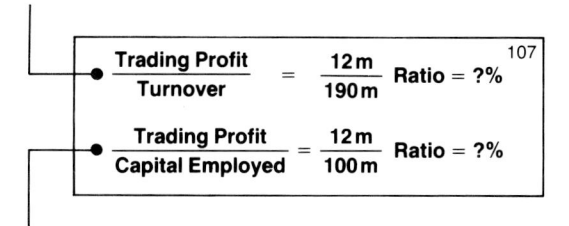

$$\frac{\text{Trading Profit}}{\text{Turnover}} = \frac{12m}{190m} \quad \text{Ratio} = ?\%$$

$$\frac{\text{Trading Profit}}{\text{Capital Employed}} = \frac{12m}{100m} \quad \text{Ratio} = ?\%$$

We estimate that our return on capital employed in 1980 was 12%.

Model questions: asking about calculations

How did you get this result?
What are your figures for return on capital employed?
What do your calculations for the European market show?
What's our current profit to turnover ratio?
Can you give me the estimates for the Small Unit sector?

Follow-up

Here is an example of the questions and answers which might follow this section of the presentation.

Further questions from the Sales and Marketing Director

The Sales and Marketing Director, Sheila Appleton, asks some questions about Hamilton's general approach to Visitron's problems.

APPLETON: *Can I ask a general question here?* You used a well known product matrix in your presentation. *Isn't there a danger that* this approach may overemphasise the marketing aspects of Visitron's problems?
HAMILTON: I think I know what you're getting at Mrs Appleton.
APPLETON: *Well, let's be frank* . . . it is conventional wisdom that consultancies are very good at analysing a company's external problems but very bad at understanding its internal problems . . .
HAMILTON: *What exactly do you mean by* 'internal problems'?
APPLETON: *I'm referring particularly to* the problem of changing attitudes.
HAMILTON: Ah . . . in that case *I tend to agree with you*. Internal company cultures are vitally important and it is very difficult for an outsider to understand how they work. *To go back to your original question* however, we believe that this company must first of all find out what the customer wants before it begins to change itself internally . . .
APPLETON: But *suppose that* the er . . . internal culture, as you called it . . . suppose that this prevented a change towards a market-oriented company?
HAMILTON: *If this were the case* then management would have to take very strong action within the company even if it meant a period of . . . how shall I put it . . . readjustment?
APPLETON: Do you mean 'conflict'?
HAMILTON: *I really don't think it's for me to comment* on this Mrs Appleton since management aspects of the problem were not part of my brief.
APPLETON: Nevertheless Mr Hamilton your recommendations could have serious implications for management systems and structures?
HAMILTON: Undoubtedly. In the final analysis however it's up to management to make sure that the change of direction is accepted by everyone.
APPLETON: You know what they say about supertankers . . .
HAMILTON: Of course it will take time to change course. All the more reason that we start turning the wheel now.

Questions and answers: language analysis

The gambits and phrases in italics above are explained below in terms of their communicative functions in the dialogue.

The black arrows represent the people asking the questions and the white arrows the people replying to them.

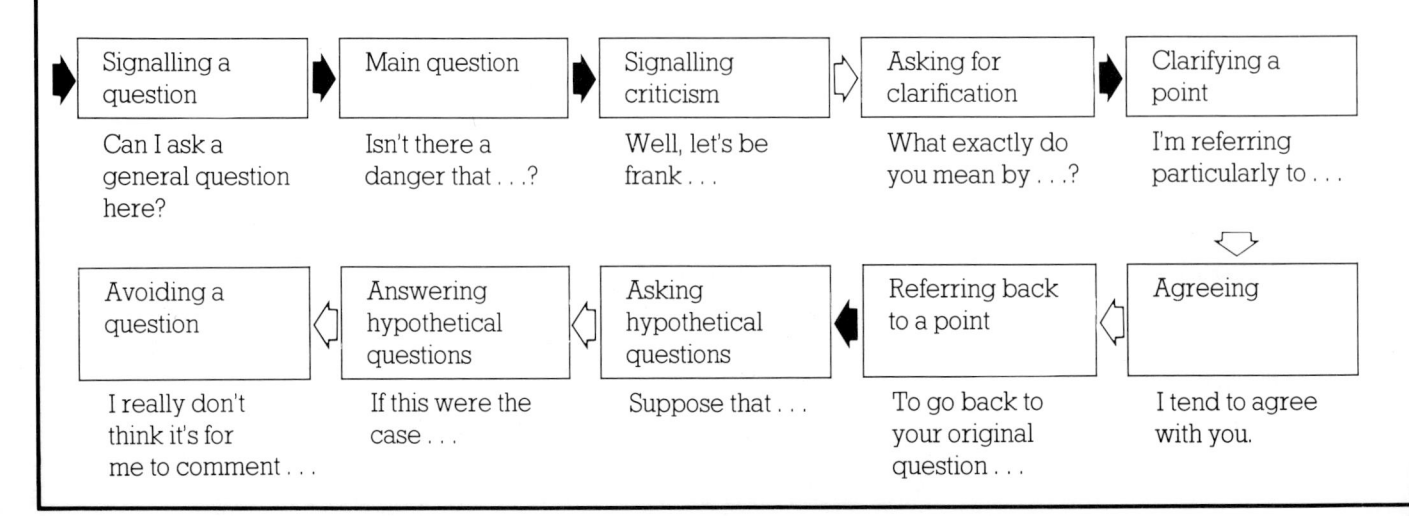

Signalling a question	Main question	Signalling criticism	Asking for clarification	Clarifying a point
Can I ask a general question here?	Isn't there a danger that . . .?	Well, let's be frank . . .	What exactly do you mean by . . .?	I'm referring particularly to . . .

Avoiding a question	Answering hypothetical questions	Asking hypothetical questions	Referring back to a point	Agreeing
I really don't think it's for me to comment . . .	If this were the case . . .	Suppose that . . .	To go back to your original question . . .	I tend to agree with you.

UNIT 12
Presenting options – 2

Preview

Language points

Hamilton now presents the remaining options.

Prescribing and predicting

... ought to ...
... should ...
... may ...
... might ...

Developing the argument – 2

For years now ...
Now however
Since then therefore
Recently though ...

Choosing to choose?
(infinitive or -ing form)

Option C proposes relocating ...

Presentation points and preview questions

Although Hamilton has a lot of information to present in the last part of his presentation, he makes his points as briefly as possible and uses the visual aid to illustrate and clarify any important concepts. To avoid unnecessary details he refers his audience to the written proposals which he presents – in a nicely designed brochure – at the end of his options. He clearly anticipates that any full discussion of these proposals can only take place after his audience has had time to digest the full written details.

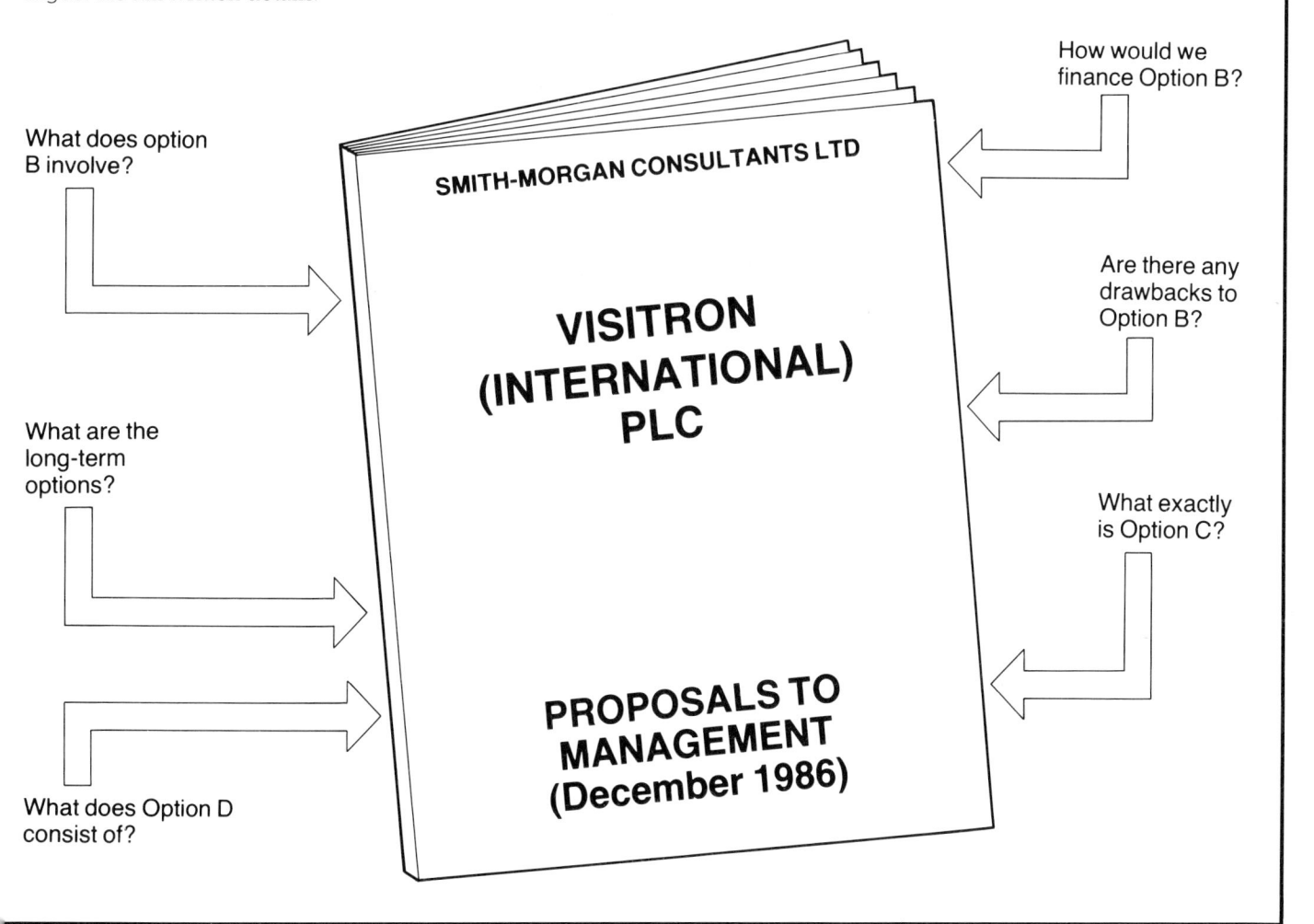

SMITH-MORGAN CONSULTANTS LTD

VISITRON (INTERNATIONAL) PLC

PROPOSALS TO MANAGEMENT (December 1986)

- What does option B involve?
- What are the long-term options?
- What does Option D consist of?
- How would we finance Option B?
- Are there any drawbacks to Option B?
- What exactly is Option C?

Summary and quick reference

12.1 Prescribing and predicting

Advice	Visitron	should ought to	reduce its prices immediately in all sectors.
Obligation	Visitron	must has to	increase its productivity if it is to survive.
Possibility	Visitron	may might	go out of business if action is not taken now.
Probability	Visitron	should ought to	survive if management accepts Hamilton's recommendations.

12.2 Developing the argument – 2

Contrast + time	Six months ago Visitron dominated the Large Unit sector.	Since then though Today, however Recently though Now, however		the situation has changed dramatically.	
		But following that Two months ago, however		the situation changed dramatically.	
Emphasis + time	Furthermore, it now In addition, it then	seems likely that seemed likely that	things	are were	going to get worse.
Result + time	So now Thus at the moment		we are taking radical action.		
	Since then therefore		we have taken radical action.		

12.3 Choosing to choose? (Infinitive or -ing form)

Infinitive of purpose: *To go* abroad you need a passport.

-ing form with prepositions: You will learn *by studying* harder.

Verbs followed by infinitive	agree arrange ask forget promise refuse seem want decide
Verbs followed by -ing form	avoid consider enjoy involve mention risk
Verbs followed by -ing form *or* infinitive	like love hate start remember begin try prefer propose

12.1 Examples from the video

```
• Advise your colleague    ▶  take a holiday          110
• Predict possibility      ▶  salary rise
• Predict probability      ▶  take-off at 6 pm
  What do these mean?  🚭  ⊘  (70)
```

You *ought to* take a holiday.
We *may get* a salary rise this year.
We *should be taking off* at 6 pm.

You *must not smoke*.
You *must keep* right.
You *must not exceed* 70 m.p.h.

Model questions: asking about advice, possibility, probability

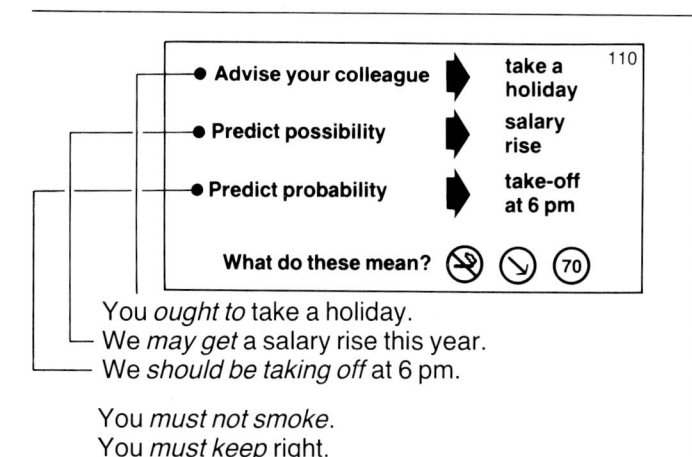

Advice:
What should we do?
What ought we to do?
Obligation:
What must we do?
What do we have to do?
Possibility:
What may happen?
What might happen?
Probability:
When should we be taking off?
Shouldn't we be in profit by now?

12.2 Examples from the video

```
Britain has been an oil importer/           113
Everything is different/She is
producing more oil than she needs/
New oil fields have been found/
There is a surplus of oil/
Britain is a major exporter of oil.

Rewrite with the following:
Since 1900/Now/Recently/Now/
At the moment/However/Thus/
So/Furthermore.
```

Since 1900 Britain has been an oil importer. *Now, however*, everything is different. *At the moment* she is producing more oil than she needs. *Recently, furthermore*, new oil fields have been found *so* there is *now* a surplus of oil. *Thus* Britain is now a major exporter of oil.

Model questions: asking about lines of argument

What evidence have you got for that?
How do you justify that statement?
Where's the evidence for that conclusion?
What other evidence have you got to support that conclusion?
How did you reach that conclusion?

12.3 Examples from the video

```
Verb +         agree/arrange/ask/           117
infinitive     forget/promise/refuse/
               seem/want/decide
Verb + -ing    avoid/consider/enjoy/
               involve/mention/risk
Verb + -ing    like/love/hate/start/
or infinitive  remember/begin/
               try/prefer/propose
```

He *agreed to do* the job when I *promised to raise* his salary.

I *considered accepting* the contract after he *mentioned cancelling* the penalty clause.

I *like playing* football.
I *like to play* football as often as possible.

Model questions: asking questions using -*ing* form or infinitives

What did you agree to do?
When did you arrange to meet?
How did you avoid seeing him?
Why did you risk losing the deal?
Do you remember seeing the letter?
Did you remember to write the letter?

Follow-up

Here is an example of the questions and answers which might follow this section of the presentation.

Questions from the Chairman and the Personnel Director

The Chairman, Sir David Stokes and the Personnel Director, Jean Macbride, question Hamilton about Option B.

SIR DAVID:	*Can we get back to more specific points? I'd like to look more closely at* Option B. You are proposing a relaunch of the Small Unit machine in two versions. *Do you think that* many customers will pay 20 per cent more for a machine which is basically the same as the lower priced version?
HAMILTON:	In a word – Yes. You still have considerable brand loyalty among some Small Unit customers... especially the private clinics. *We think* we can keep those customers with the high priced version and at the same time penetrate the public sector with the lower priced model.
SIR DAVID:	*You don't think* there's any risk of cannibalising the up-market sector?
HAMILTON:	A lot depends on how we differentiate the products during the relaunch. But there's always a risk that some private customers will transfer to the cheaper version.
MACBRIDE:	*While we're talking about* Option B Mr Hamilton *could I ask a question?*
HAMILTON:	Certainly.
MACBRIDE:	*You mentioned* job losses resulting from the changeover to the new sales system. *Can you be more specific?*
HAMILTON:	*Well by* changing over to the dealer franchise system we expect a 40 per cent reduction in our present sales staff. *However* some of this will be absorbed by the transfer of some of those people to the Large Unit division. *In addition to this* our proposals recommend that existing sales staff be allowed to bid for the franchises. *In the final analysis* then I think we're talking about job losses of about 25–30 per cent of the sales force.
MACBRIDE:	That's not to mention the losses that would result from relocation.
HAMILTON:	That's a completely different question.
MACBRIDE:	Even so the immediate losses will mean large redundancy payments and a loss of morale.
HAMILTON:	*I'm afraid so.* But let's look on the positive side. It will also mean great opportunities for the people who bid for the franchises and, of course, a much brighter future for those who stay in Visitron.

Questions and answers: language analysis

The gambits and phrases in italics above are explained below in terms of their communicative functions in the dialogue.

The black arrows represent the people asking the questions and the white arrows the people replying to them.

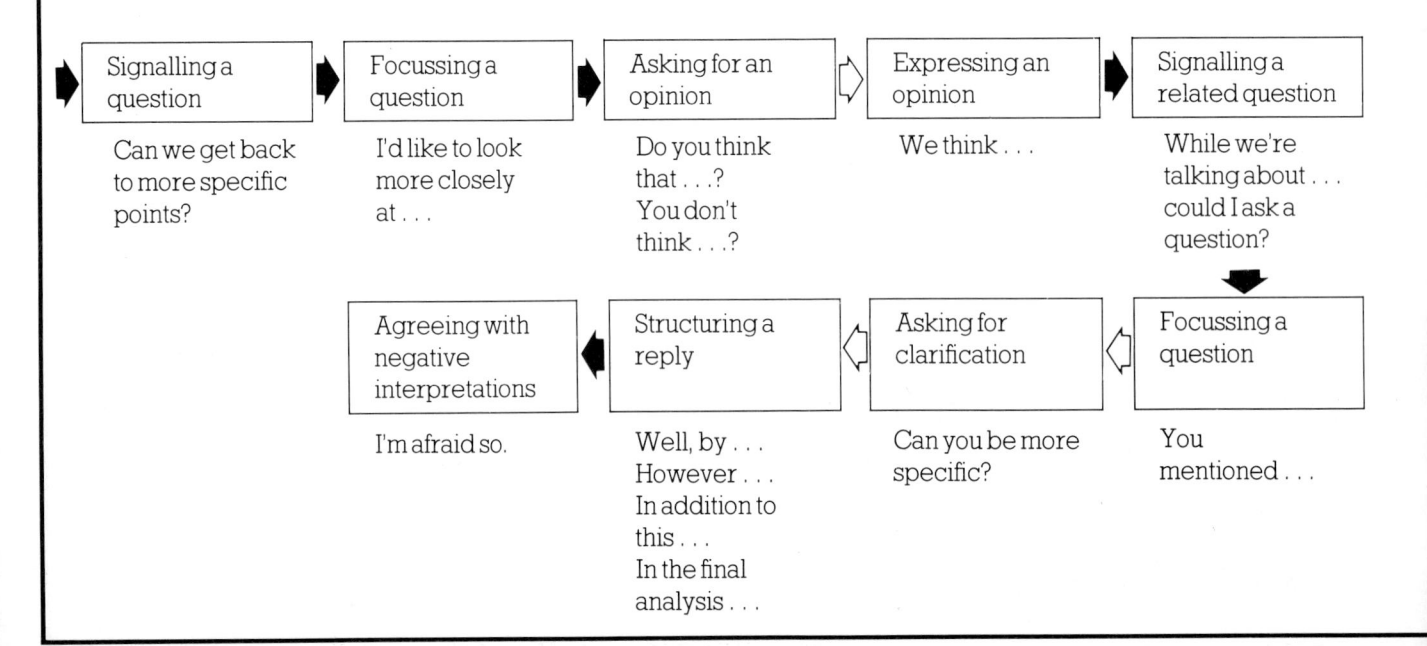

Signalling a question	Focussing a question	Asking for an opinion	Expressing an opinion	Signalling a related question
Can we get back to more specific points?	I'd like to look more closely at...	Do you think that...? You don't think...?	We think...	While we're talking about... could I ask a question?

	Agreeing with negative interpretations	Structuring a reply	Asking for clarification	Focussing a question
	I'm afraid so.	Well, by... However... In addition to this... In the final analysis...	Can you be more specific?	You mentioned...

UNIT 13
Presenting recommendations

Preview

Language points

Hamilton eliminates one of the options he has just described and then presents and justifies his recommendations.

Justifying decisions	*Eliminating alternatives*	*Making recommendations*
Because of . . .	We rule out . . .	We strongly urge . . .
Owing to . . .	We reject . . .	We recommend that . . .

Presentation points and preview questions

Hamilton now delivers the recommendations for which his team was commissioned. Since he has already presented the advantages and disadvantages of the various options very carefully, most of his audience know what is coming. Hamilton is therefore very brief and to the point. All the controversial elements have been introduced and argued during earlier stages of the presentation and so the final recommendations do not shock or offend. To end on a positive and forward looking note he puts all the recommendations into the context of a five year planning map.

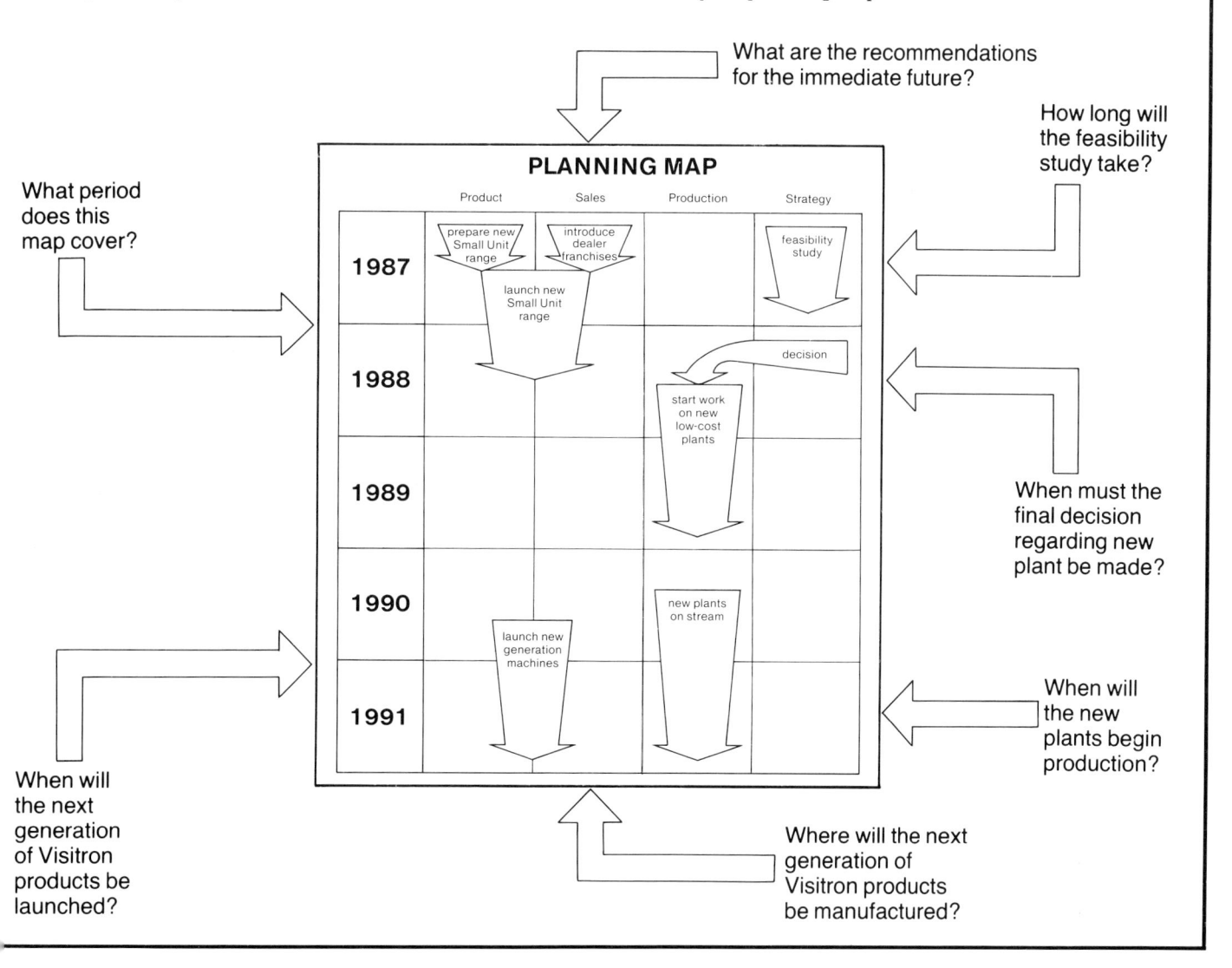

PLANNING MAP

What are the recommendations for the immediate future?

How long will the feasibility study take?

What period does this map cover?

When must the final decision regarding new plant be made?

When will the new plants begin production?

When will the next generation of Visitron products be launched?

Where will the next generation of Visitron products be manufactured?

Planning map columns: Product, Sales, Production, Strategy

- 1987: prepare new Small Unit range; introduce dealer franchises; feasibility study; launch new Small Unit range
- 1988: decision; start work on new low-cost plants
- 1989:
- 1990: new plants on stream
- 1991: launch new generation machines

49

Summary and quick reference

13.1 Justifying decisions

Because of Owing to Since there is As a result of	a rise in demand,	we have increased output.
Demand is up.	For this reason	we have increased output.
We have increased output.	The reason for this is	a rise in demand.
We have increased output	because of	

13.2 Eliminating alternatives

We rule out We have eliminated We have decided against We reject	Option A	because of the marginal savings it would give us.
We accept We have chosen We have selected We have decided to adopt	Option B	because of the clear benefits it would give in the overall market.

13.3 Making recommendations

We strongly urge	that	this year's dividend	is
We recommend			be
			should be	increased.
We recommend We would recommend We urge	an increase		in this year's dividend.
We think you should . . . You ought to . . .	increase		this year's dividend.

13.1 Examples from the video

I decided to learn English *because of* the number of international meetings I must attend.

> 1. Your decision to learn English.[120]
> 2. The decision to send men to the moon.
> 3. The decision to increase factory automation.

Men were sent to the moon *because of* the need for knowledge, experience and scientific advance.

Model questions: asking about decisions

What have you decided?
What is your decision?
Why did you make this decision?
Why did you decide this?
Why did you decide to learn English?
How do you justify this decision?

13.2 Examples from the video

Package Holidays			[123]
Barbados	**Miami**	**Cuba**	
10 days	9 days	21 days	
£700	£300	£275	
Breakfast & lunch	Breakfast & dinner	All meals	
Own room	Own room	Share room	

I have decided against Barbados because it is too expensive. *I have also ruled out* the holiday in Cuba since I would have to share a room. *I have therefore chosen* the holiday in Miami because it is the best value for money.

Model questions: asking about alternatives

What are our options?
What are the alternatives?
What options do we have?
What choice do we have?
Why did you decide against this alternative?
Why didn't you choose this option?
Why do you rule out the first option?
Why have you decided to adopt this alternative?

13.3 Examples from the video

		[126]
Turnover	212,500,000	
Pre-tax profit	949,000	
Funds employed	110,700,000	
• Borrowings	12,120,000	
• Earnings per share	2.86p	

I would recommend that Visitron increases its borrowings in order to purchase new plant.

With such low earnings per share *I don't think you should* invest in Visitron at the moment.

Model questions: asking about recommendations

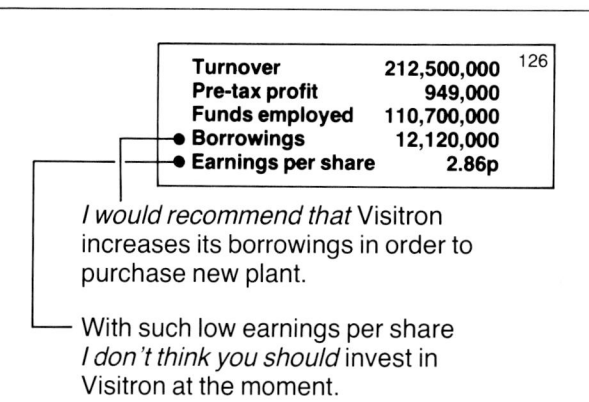

What are your recommendations?
What do you recommend?
What would you recommend?
What do you think we should do?
What does Hamilton think that Visitron ought to do?
What would you do in this situation?

Follow-up

Here is an example of the questions and answers which might follow this section of the presentation.

Further questions from the Production Director

Robert Scott, Visitron's Production Director, asks for more information about the future of the Medium and Large Unit machines.

HAMILTON: *Any more questions ladies and gentlemen?*
SCOTT: Yes. You made no specific mention of the Medium and Large Unit products in your recommendations. *What future do you see for* these machines in the medium and long term?
HAMILTON: Mm... *that's an interesting question. There are two main imponderables here. Firstly* we are not sure how the growth of networking will affect the sales of Large Unit machines. At the moment some Large Unit users have changed over to networked Small Unit machines. They say they get greater flexibility at lower cost. If this trend continues it could have a big effect on Large Unit sales. *Secondly* however we're not sure when the hologram facility will be ready for the market. If it comes soon it could revolutionise the Large Unit machines' future. *One interpretation of* the present move to networked Small Unit machines is that Large Unit customers are delaying their purchasing decisions to see what will happen to hologram research.
SCOTT: *Do you believe that?*
HAMILTON: It makes some sense.
SCOTT: *In other words* we're seeing only a short-term decline in the Large and Medium Unit sectors?
HAMILTON: We certainly can't write off the larger machines yet.
SCOTT: And what do we do in those divisions while we wait for the situation to become clearer?
HAMILTON: Our proposals contain detailed recommendations for R&D. *In a nutshell* we're suggesting accelerated research into both networking systems and holography. *In addition* there should be rapid development of a hand held scanner for the mid-90s.
SCOTT: A very expensive and ambitious programme.
HAMILTON: Yes... but then the stakes are very high.

Questions and answers: language analysis

The gambits and phrases in italics above are explained below in terms of their communicative functions in the dialogue.

The black arrows represent the people asking the questions and the white arrows the people replying to them.

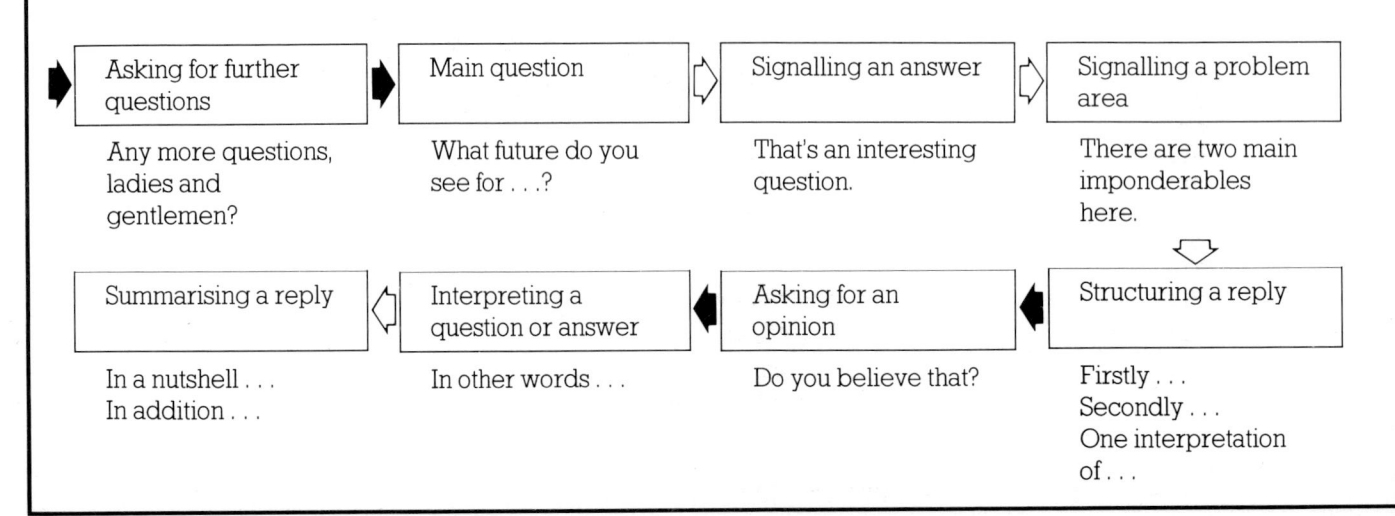

Asking for further questions	Main question	Signalling an answer	Signalling a problem area
Any more questions, ladies and gentlemen?	What future do you see for...?	That's an interesting question.	There are two main imponderables here.

Summarising a reply	Interpreting a question or answer	Asking for an opinion	Structuring a reply
In a nutshell... In addition...	In other words...	Do you believe that?	Firstly... Secondly... One interpretation of...

UNIT 14
Ending the presentation

Preview

Language points

Hamilton sums up his central argument and concludes with a challenge to his audience. He closes his presentation by inviting questions.

Summing up	Concluding	Closing
To sum up then . . .	I'd like to conclude . . .	Thank you . . . you no doubt have
Let me now just recap . . .	Let me end by saying . . .	many questions . . .

Presentation points and preview questions

Hamilton ends on a positive and dynamic note. He has to show that he has completed his original brief. He also has to encourage his audience to take the right action in the future. To do this he summarises his presentation in three parts. Firstly he presents a colourful picture of the present dangers. Secondly he explains in one sentence how those dangers can be avoided and thirdly he presents a challenge to his audience. To end his presentation on a memorable note he is very brief and uses images rather than detailed sentences. He ends by inviting questions from the audience.

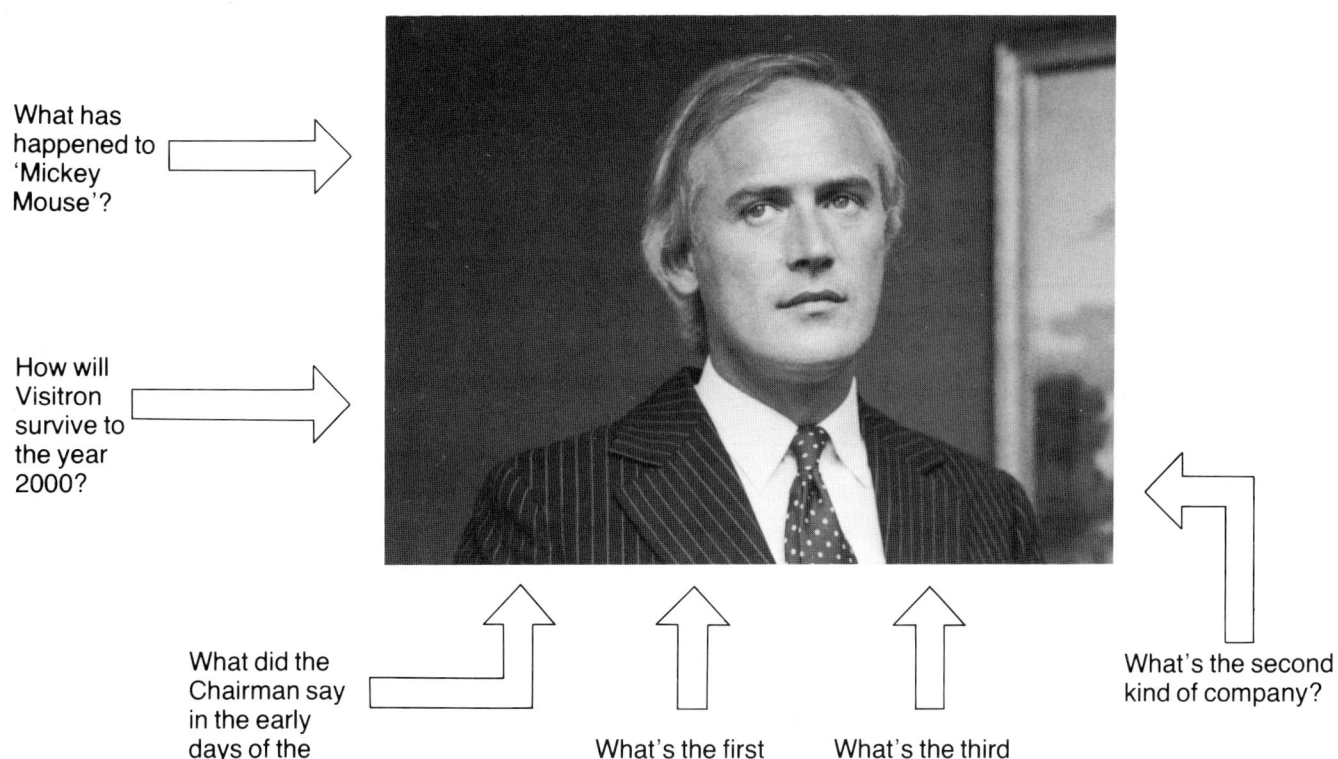

What has happened to 'Mickey Mouse'?

How will Visitron survive to the year 2000?

What did the Chairman say in the early days of the company?

What's the first kind of company?

What's the third kind of company?

What's the second kind of company?

53

Summary and quick reference

14.1 Summing up

To sum up then To summarise my main points To recapitulate then	Visitron must reduce its production costs and become more market-oriented.
Let me now sum up. Let me now just recap.	Firstly Visitron must reduce its production costs and secondly it must become more market-oriented.

14.2 Concluding

I'd like to conclude Let me end I'd like to finish	by reminding	you of something your Chairman said in the highly successful early days of this company.
In conclusion Finally,	may I remind	

14.3 Closing

Thank you. You no doubt have many questions.
If there are any questions I shall do my best to answer them.
I'm sure you have many questions.

14.1 Examples from the video

```
                                    129
  1. Visitron uncompetitive
  2. No new products in pipeline
  3. Must become market-oriented
  4. Must cut production costs
```

Right then. *Let me now sum up.* Firstly there is no doubt that Visitron's prices are uncompetitive. Secondly we have no new products in the pipeline and thirdly we must clearly become more market-oriented. Finally, however, our long-term aim must be to cut production costs.

Model questions: asking about summaries

Could you summarise your main points please?
Could you recap on that?
I wonder if you could recapitulate your main points please?
How would you summarise your main argument?
How would you sum up the main problem?

14.2 Examples from the video

```
                                    132
  1. Economy growing
  2. Inflation falling
  3. Demand rising
  4. We have the right products ↓
  5. _____
```

To sum up then, the economy is growing, inflation is falling at the same time as demand is rising and finally we have got the right products. *In conclusion I would say that we must not miss this opportunity to win more orders than ever before.*

Model questions: asking about concluding remarks

What's your conclusion?
In conclusion, what would you say is the main problem?
You finished by saying we must become more market-oriented. What exactly do you mean by that?
In your concluding remarks, what did you mean by, '......'?

14.3 Examples from the video

```
                                    135
        Thank you
    I'd like to conclude . . .
```

There are those that make things happen. Those that watch things happen. And there are those that wonder what happened. Gentlemen . . . we must start to make things happen now. *Thank you. If there are any questions I shall do my best to answer them . . .*

Model questions: asking about the question session

Do you object if we ask questions?
Would you object if we asked questions?
May I begin the questions?
Could I start the questions?
May we ask questions during the presentation?

Follow-up

Here is an example of the questions and answers which might follow this section of the presentation.

Final questions and thanks from the Chairman

The Chairman of Visitron, Sir David Stokes, asks one last question and then brings the question and answer session to a close by thanking Richard Hamilton on behalf of the audience and the company.

SIR DAVID: *Unless there are any more questions* I think this is a good time to finish ladies and gentlemen . . . *Perhaps before we break Richard I could ask one last* general question myself?

HAMILTON: Please do Sir David.

SIR DAVID: Today you have recommended a dramatic change of corporate direction for this company. Many people will be worried about the risks and dangers involved. *What would you say* to those people?

HAMILTON: I would say, Sir David, that business is about risk. You took a risk when you invested your money in magnetic scanning research. It might have failed. Fortunately for everyone here it didn't. Your competitors took risks when they entered the market in '72 and '73. Unfortunately for everyone here they did *not* fail. I would draw the following lesson. If you can't remember the last big risk that you or your company took, then you and your company are in for a very big surprise . . . in the very near future . . .

SIR DAVID: OK. But there are risks and risks Richard. You have recommended a major relocation, a big push into a difficult market and a total change in our sales policy . . . all in a short period of time. Some people might say we should be more cautious.

HAMILTON: *Don't misunderstand me.* Visitron still has many great strengths which must be maintained. We are recommending corporate evolution not corporate revolution Sir David . . .

SIR DAVID: I have no doubt of that Richard. I imagine however that some of us here thought that evolution was a slower and more gradual process.

HAMILTON: In some cases it was Sir David. And in some of those cases too slow to save the creature from extinction . . .

SIR DAVID: Yes . . . well . . . I . . . er . . . think you've made your point Richard. *Perhaps on that note we should end.* Could I remind everyone that we meet again for the financial presentation at 2.30 this afternoon? *It* now *remains for me to thank you,* Richard, *on behalf of* everyone here, for a very thorough and useful presentation . . .

Questions and answers: language analysis

The gambits and phrases in italics above are explained below in terms of their communicative functions in the dialogue.

The black arrows represent the people asking the questions and the white arrows the people replying to them.

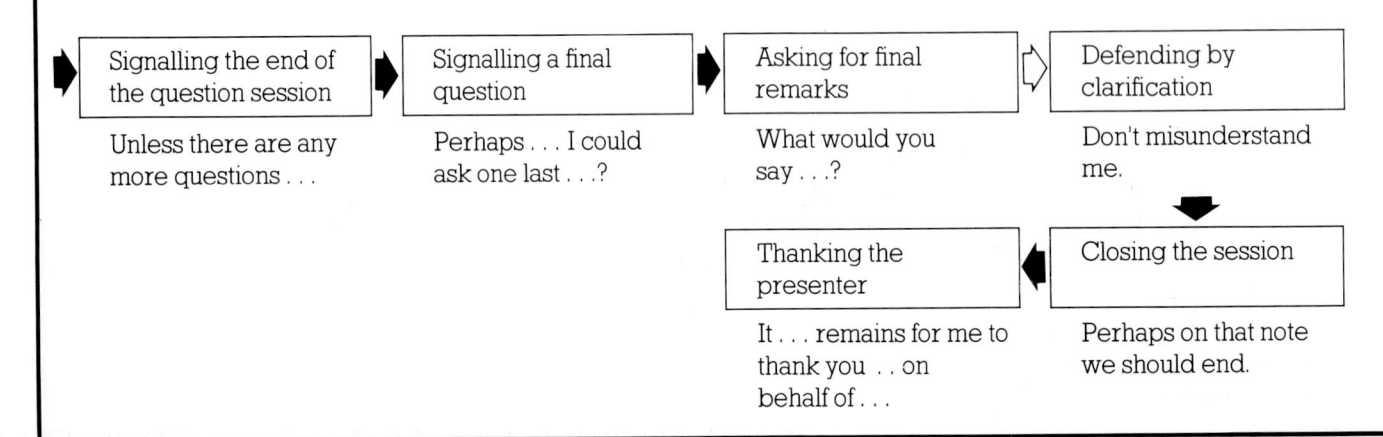

Signalling the end of the question session	Signalling a final question	Asking for final remarks	Defending by clarification
Unless there are any more questions . . .	Perhaps . . . I could ask one last . . . ?	What would you say . . . ?	Don't misunderstand me.

		Thanking the presenter	Closing the session
		It . . . remains for me to thank you . . on behalf of . . .	Perhaps on that note we should end.

Questions and answers: language analysis index

This section identifies the language items that will help you to organise question and answer sessions, ask questions and give answers. You can see each phrase or sentence in context by turning to the page number indicated.

1 Organising the question and answer session

a)	*Starting the questions*	You no doubt have many questions...	
		If there are any questions...	
		I'm sure you have many questions...	54
b)	*Asking for further questions*	Any more questions ladies and gentlemen?	52
c)	*Ending the questions*	Unless there are any more questions...	56
d)	*Closing the session*	Perhaps on that note we should end.	56
e)	*Thanking*	It remains for me to thank you on behalf of...	56

2 Asking questions

You can find examples of direct questions on the Summary and quick reference pages of each unit of this Handbook. In presentations or meetings however, asking questions is often a little more complicated. Because there are many people in a meeting, a person has to first of all get peoples' attention by *signalling* that he has a question. He must then identify the general area of his question by *focussing* it. Finally he can ask his direct question.

a)	*Signalling the first question*	Perhaps I could begin the questions...?	4
b)	*Signalling a question*	Excuse me...	12
		Mr Hamilton.	20
		Could I come in here...?	8
		I'd like to ask you about...	16
		I have a question about...	28
		Can I ask a general question here?	44
		I wonder if we could go on to...?	40
c)	*Signalling a following question*	This leads me on to another question...	28
		One last question...	40
		Perhaps I could ask one last...?	56
		Let me put another point to you.	32
		But surely...?	12
		There's just one further question.	24
d)	*Signalling a related question*	While we're on this subject...	16
		While we're talking about...	48
e)	*Focussing a question*	Could we go back to...?	4, 12
		It seems to me that...	8
		You mentioned...	24, 48
		I'd like to look more closely at...	48
f)	*Signalling and focussing critical questions*	I want to take you up on...	20
		Can I be quite frank with you?	32
		I'm a little worried about...	12
		Are you aware that...?	28
		I'd like to take issue with you...	24

g)	*Examples of some main questions*	Can you tell me how you arrived at...?	16
		Then wouldn't you say...?	28
		My question is whether...?	12, 40
		What about...?	40
		Isn't there a danger that...?	44
		What future do you see for...?	52
h)	*Dealing with an interruption*	Sorry... Could I just finish?	24
i)	*Asking for an opinion*	Do you think that...?	48
		Do you believe that?	52
		Don't you think...?	4
j)	*Asking for clarification*	What exactly do you mean by...?	20, 44
		Could you be more specific?	28
		In what sense...?	40
		Does this also mean that...?	16
		How do you mean?	12
k)	*Asking a multiple question*	What is... and why exactly...?	8
l)	*Asking for examples*	For example?	4, 28
m)	*Asking hypothetical questions*	Supposing...?	40
		Suppose that...	44
n)	*Insisting on an answer*	You still haven't answered my question...	20

3 Giving answers

Answers can have many different functions. They can agree or disagree with a statement. They can provide information. They can indicate attitudes. They can support the flow of a discussion or they can challenge the flow of a discussion. The way you answer a question depends on many different factors. Below is a general description of the functions of some typical phrases.

a)	*Signalling an answer*	That's an interesting question.	52
		It's a good question...	40
b)	*Rephrasing a question*	If I understand you correctly you're saying that...	20
		In other words...	52
c)	*Making a point*	The fact is that...	4, 20
		My point was that...	32, 36
		My point is that...	8
		Could I just point out that...	24
		I think that only proves... point.	36
d)	*Conceding a point before making a point*	I would agree that... Nevertheless...	4
		Yes... but surely...	8
		Of course. My point is though...	8
		I admit that... However...	8
		Of course, but...	28
		I take your point... However...	24
		Certainly, but...	28
		Of course they were. I agree... Nevertheless...	32
e)	*Dismissing a point before making a point*	Even so... wouldn't you agree that...?	4
		Be that as it may...	28
		That may be so... But surely...	4
f)	*Signalling disagreement*	With respect...	4
		With all due respect...	20
		To be quite frank...	28
		Well let's be frank...	44
g)	*Rejecting a point*	I understand your concern. It's our view, however...	24
h)	*Signalling rejection of a criticism*	Can I just say something in defence of...	36
i)	*Referring back to a point*	I'd also like to remind you of...	24
		As I said before...	28
		To go back to your original question...	44

j)	Agreeing with a point	I agree...	12
		I'm afraid so.	48
k)	Disagreeing with a point	Not exactly...	40
l)	Defending a point	Let me put my remarks into a proper perspective.	36
		You may be interested to know that...	36
m)	Clarifying a point	What I was trying to say... was...	4
		I mean that...	20
		Don't misunderstand me...	24, 56
		Please don't get me wrong...	32
		You're referring to...	36
		I'm referring particularly to...	44
n)	Structuring an answer	Firstly... Secondly... Thirdly...	8, 52
		On the demand side... On the supply side	16
		In the short run... In the long run...	16
		It gave us... What it did not give us...was...	32
		Well first of all... furthermore however...	32
		Most importantly though...	32
		Well by... however... in addition to this...	
		In the final analysis...	48
o)	Answering multiple questions	I think there are three separate questions there...	8
		Let me begin with your first point... As far as your second question is concerned... With respect to your final question...	8
p)	Expressing opinions	I would say that...	4
		We think...	48
		In our view...	4
		I feel that...	36
		It seems to me that...	8, 32
q)	Answering hypothetical questions	If this were the case...	44
r)	Giving examples	For example...	28
s)	Inferring and asking about inference	Does this also mean that...?	16
t)	Adding information	Something I did not mention earlier is that...	16
		I should also add that...	40
		You may be interested to know that...	36
		Let me add immediately...	36
u)	Putting a different point of view	Looking at it from another point of view...	20
		Let me put another point to you...	32
v)	Breaking off	OK. Perhaps I'm splitting hairs.	12
		OK... We can discuss this later.	24
w)	Summarising	In a nutshell...	52
x)	Avoiding a question	I really don't think it's for me to comment...	44

Some practical tips on giving presentations

Below are some practical suggestions on how to prepare and deliver presentations. They are designed to help you construct and practise your own presentation in a logical and methodical manner.

The key to an effective presentation is the establishment of high audience interest or receptivity. You should therefore aim to present your ideas clearly, quickly and attractively. Make sure for example that your presentation has a beginning, a middle and an end. Make sure also that there is a progression of content which builds up an audience's interest to a central point, message or event. In other words, your presentation should have the three main ingredients for successful communication: content, shape and direction.

Before the presentation: preparation

Careful preparation will help you to improve your presentation dramatically. There are three stages of preparation:

Stage 1 Focussing

* Make sure you have enough time to prepare effectively.
* Clarify your terms of reference.
* Establish your objectives clearly in your own mind.
* Find out exactly who your audience will be.
* Try to see your presentation in its widest context. Is it the beginning of a new company policy? Is it a small part of something bigger?
* Try to predict probable audience reaction.
* Choose the best way of speaking to your audience, e.g. briefly and directly or carefully and methodically.

Stage 2 Building

* Collect your materials. Identify the limits of your subject.
* Choose the key materials. Reject unimportant materials.
* Establish a clear idea of what you want to say. Convince yourself before you try to convince your audience.
* Identify your key points and if possible reduce each one to a single sentence.
* Put each key point into its natural order and establish a direction which will lead to your central point, message or event.
* Memorise the sequence of key points and practise speaking them out aloud without looking at notes.
* Stand back and try to see the profile of your presentation. Do you give away too much too quickly? Do the points build up to your central point?
* Decide what visual aids will help your audience to understand your main points.
* Decide what information these visual aids should and should not include.
* Sketch the visual aids and position them within the sequence of points you have established so far.

Stage 3 Polishing

* Begin writing clear and readable notes. Develop your own symbols or shorthand.
* Finalise your structure in the form of an agenda or overview.
* Make sure you have a good beginning. In other words make sure you establish your audience's interest as early as possible. How you do this depends on the situation. In some cases a joke may be appropriate. In other cases it will be enough to refer to a major problem or opportunity.
* Practise delivery of your central point or message.
* Identify any statements that could be improved by changing them into rhetorical questions. Rhetorical questions raise audience attention. They also provide useful introductions to new topics or subject areas.
* Write into your notes the minimum extra information that you will need to support each point.
* Finish your visual aids. Make sure there are signals for them in your notes. Practise your lead-ins to the visual aids.
* Check the length and timing of each section.
* Finish your notes on clearly numbered cards or pages and make sure these are securely held in order.
* Rehearse main points together with visual aids.
* Check all hardware is working and that you can use it quickly and efficiently. Arrange alternative hardware in case of breakdowns.
* Check location of presentation, seating arrangements, time, etc.

During the presentation

Before beginning try to see yourself as your audience will see you. Avoid mannerisms. Don't forget the importance of appearance and voice. Remember the positive aspects of nerves. They mean you are sensitive to your audience, ready to think quickly and that you are not overconfident!

* Make sure there is a proper introduction.
* Present your terms of reference briefly and as early as possible.
* Be sensitive to your audience's reactions from the start. Guide your audience carefully.
* Present your structure by means of an agenda or overview.
* Keep to your structure but be flexible within it according to audience reaction.
* Signal the various stages of your structure. Tell your audience when you have finished one section and are going on to the next. It helps to give a sense of control, order and direction.
* Present your less important points early and briefly.
* Summarise and repeat where it will help and build towards your more important points and central message.
* Don't say too much. Don't make things too complicated.
* Remember the value of visual aids as a change of focus for the audience and a source of valuable thinking time for you.
* Enjoy showing your visual aids. Stand close to them without blocking the view. Point boldly to their important features. Cover them when you have finished with them to prevent later audience distraction.
* Introduce and develop controversial points early. Don't leave them until the end.
* Make sure your presentation moves quickly and logically.
* Refer to notes quickly and not too often. Don't become over dependent on them.
* Make sure all your points come together in the key issue or message. Present this message clearly, attractively and at greater length if necessary.
* Summarise your key message.
* End effectively. Refer back to your original aims or brief and show your audience that you have achieved or fulfilled them. End on a note which is both positive and memorable.

After the presentation: questions and answers

This stage of the presentation session is usually marked by a change of relationship between presenter and audience. The audience will now have a chance to participate directly. You will have a chance to relax slightly and also to gain more thinking time. Exploit this slight change of relationship. Stand back from your presentation and see it some extent like an artist would see his finished painting. In other words move a little towards your audience's point of view. Your apparent objectivity will make it easier to handle questions.

* Take a more relaxed posture if appropriate. Move physically closer to your audience if possible.
* Try to control the question and answer session by anticipating questions and moving your answers towards other anticipated questions.
* Listen to the questions. If they are not clear rephrase them.
* Make sure your answers are as simple and brief as possible. Don't invite trouble!
* Try to enjoy the questions. Relax and introduce humour if possible and appropriate.
* Concede points if necessary.
* Admit ignorance if necessary. Don't bluff.
* Refer back to structure or content of original presentation. This will reinforce sense of completeness and plan.
* Maintain appearance of objectivity towards your own presentation. Don't be aggressive. Don't be emotional. Be generous to criticisms.
* Identify yourself clearly with good points from the audience.
* Refer questioners to other sources or persons when appropriate.
* Refer back to your terms of reference if a question is outside your brief.
* Finish by presenting a summary of your presentation plus any points which have come up during the question and answer session.

Glossary

In this glossary you will find short definitions of the specialised business vocabulary used in the video and the dialogues in this Handbook. For further information refer to a source such as the *Longman Dictionary of Business English*.

assets	all things owned by a company e.g. factories, offices, vehicles, equipment.
acquisition	the purchase or takeover of one company by another company.
balance sheet	the overall statement of a company's financial position at a particular date. It usually consists of two sections. Liabilities on the left show where finance comes from. Assets on the right show how the finance is used.
balance of trade	the difference between the visible imports of a country and the visible exports expressed in money terms.
book value	the value of the assets of a company as shown in its accounts.
borrowings	long-term loans to a company from banks or other sources.
break-even	to be in a position where revenue from sales is equal to costs of production so that neither a profit nor a loss is made.
budget overruns	the amount by which expenditure exceeds a budget target.
cannibalise	a marketing term used when the marketing strategy used to promote a particular product of a company causes the sales of another product of the same company to decline or stop completely.
capital employed	the main sources of finance for a company. It usually consists of share capital, reserves and long-term bank loans. These items usually appear on the liabilities side of the balance sheet.
cash cows	a marketing term to describe a company's most successful product. It has a high market share and does not need a lot of money to keep this position. It therefore produces a lot of cash for the company.
company plan	a long-term plan for a company's organisation and activities.
company turnaround	the conversion of a company from a loss making business to a profit making business.
competitive pricing	fixing the price of a product to gain an advantage over competitive products.
corporate strategy	a long-term strategy for a company's activities.
corporate targets	the targets which the corporate strategy tries to achieve.
contribution to overheads	the income received from the sale of a product does not always cover the total costs of producing that product. However, as long as the income exceeds the direct costs e.g. materials, fuel, there will be something left to help to cover indirect or overhead costs. This amount is called the contribution to overheads.
dealer franchise system	a sales system in which an independent dealer buys the right or franchise to sell a producer's product in one area.
demand side	anything to do with why customers want to buy things.
dividends	profits distributed to shareholders.
division	one of the more or less independent units into which a large business has been divided for purposes of management.
down-market product	a product for the poorer sections of a market.
downtime	time during which no use is made of machinery e.g. due to breakdowns, lack of materials, labour problems.

earnings per share	profits attributable to shareholders divided by the number of ordinary shares in issue.
economies of scale	the economies and therefore lower unit costs of production to be got from producing large quantities of a product.
exchange rate variations	changes in the value of one currency against another.
feasibility study	a careful analysis of a proposed new product, process or project.
fixed costs	costs that do not vary with output e.g. buildings.
high-tech	high technology.
hologram	a three-dimensional image of an object created by a special laser beam process.
holography	the rapidly developing science and technique of producing holograms.
image premium	the higher price customers will pay because of a product's or a company's reputation or image.
market coverage	the degree to which a company has products to satisfy every particular need or demand in one market.
market-oriented	a company which is sensitive to the needs of its markets rather than to its own internal needs.
market-segmentation strategy	a marketing plan which aims to divide one market into various sub-units.
market share	the proportion of a total market supplied by one product or manufacturer.
me too products	a marketing term for products of one company which imitate or copy the products of another company.
merger	when two companies combine to form one company.
Mickey Mouse operators	companies which need not be taken seriously.
negative profitability	the opposite of profit i.e. losses.
net sterling receipts	the income received from overseas sales after they have been converted to sterling and after charges, costs etc. have been deducted.
networking systems	the linking of several small computers to provide the same operational capacity as one large computer.
net worth	the difference between total assets and total liabilities. It represents the value of a business after all claims against it have been paid.
operational plan	a plan for operations rather than organisation or investment.
output per man hour	the value of output per period divided by the number of hours worked in the same period.
patent	the exclusive right to produce and sell a new invention.
payroll	the total amount paid to employees as wages and salaries.
pre-tax profits	trading profits *plus* income from other activities e.g. shares in other companies, *less* interest paid on loans.
price competition	market competition in which price is the key weapon.
product spread matrix	a diagram which compares a company's products in terms of market shares and market growth rates.
productivity gap	the difference between one company's or nation's output per man and another's.
production constraints	the factors that limit a company's ability to produce things more cheaply or more quickly.
profit and loss account	an accounting statement which calculates a company's net profit or loss.
public sector	all those industries or organisations which are run or owned by the government.
question mark products	products in the product spread matrix about which there is some uncertainty whether to spend more to promote them or to stop promoting them altogether.

R & D	research and development.
rationalisation	a planned reorganisation of a company to improve efficiency.
(in) real terms	a measure of value which is adjusted for inflation e.g. In money terms wages rose by 10 per cent. Inflation rose by 5 per cent. *In real terms*, therefore, wages rose by only 5 per cent.
redundancies	the number of workers dismissed because of lack of work.
redundancy payments	amounts paid to workers who have been made redundant to compensate them for loss of earnings.
re-launch	launching a new product for a second time in order to improve its chances of success.
relative market share	a measure used in the product spread matrix to show a product's share of a market compared with the share of the market of its nearest competitor e.g. a relative market share of 2.0 means that a product has twice the share of its closest competitive product.
reserves	amounts set aside from profits to meet future expenditure needs.
return on capital employed	trading profit divided by capital employed in a company. This very important management ratio shows the percentage profit generated by a company's capital base. It allows a company to compare its overall performance with a similar company in the same industry.
return on investment	the percentage profit that an investor will receive from a particular investment.
sales area test	the testing of a new system or product in one particular sales territory to see if it is suitable for all areas.
sales target shortfalls	the amount by which sales are below sales targets.
share capital	the amount of capital in a business which is financed by share issues.
share price	the market price of a share sold on a stock exchange.
star	a product in the product spread matrix which has a high share in a rapidly expanding market but which, because of high costs of promotion, is not yet very profitable. When the market matures however it will not need a lot of promotion and will therefore become a highly profitable cash cow.
stripped down version	a product model which has the minimum basic features.
takeover risk	the danger that a company will be bought or taken over by another company.
tariff barrier/tariff wall	import taxes or quotas designed to protect home industries from foreign competition.
technological lead	the advantage that one product or company has over another in terms of technology.
trading profits	the profits from a company's normal activities. It does not include income from shares in other companies or interest paid on long-term loans. See pre-tax profits.
turnover	total sales over a specified period.
up-graded	persuaded to replace a machine with a larger, more expensive or more modern machine from the same manufacturer.
value added per employee	this is a common measure of productivity. It is the difference between what the producer pays for his supplies and what he sells his final product for i.e. the value he adds to his raw materials and labour. This added value is then divided by the number of employees.
variable costs	costs which change depending on the volume of production.
wage bill	the total cost of wages and salaries.
zero budgeting	a budgeting system which builds up the probable costs from zero rather than from current cost levels.

Tapescript

Valerie Singleton

Hello. We're going to hear a short presentation given by an external consultant to the senior management of a British company called Visitron. Visitron produces a range of magnetic scanning machines for use in medical and industrial diagnostic units. These scanners produce perfect pictures of internal organs or material structures without being harmful to the user or to the patient.

Visitron's European market divides into three product sectors. There's the Large Unit sector which comprises major hospitals and engineering companies, and in this sector Visitron sells a large machine which can produce fifteen pictures simultaneously. In the Medium Unit sector – that's large clinics and small hospitals and medium-sized engineering companies – Visitron sells a machine which can produce up to six pictures simultaneously. The third sector is the Small Unit sector, which consists of doctors' surgeries and small firms, and in this sector Visitron sells a low-price, compact scanner which produces a single image.

In 1985 Visitron launched a new generation of scanners. Now, in late 1986, they've run into difficulties in the market, so to overcome those difficulties they've called in a top management consultant, Richard Hamilton. Let's sit in on his presentation.

1 Sir David Stokes

Right, ladies and gentlemen. For those of you who don't already know him, I'd like to introduce you to Richard Hamilton. He's on loan to us from the Smith-Morgan Consultancy. Richard . . .

Richard Hamilton

Good morning . . . er . . . four months ago, in the face of the . . . er . . . current difficulties, your Chairman requested my team to prepare a series of options and recommendations for management as a matter of priority. Briefly, Visitron's initial successes with the new scanner range in 1985 have not been sustained this year. Sales in all three sectors are down, and with the poorest pre-tax profits for many years the Visitron share price is dangerously low. What is more, our projections to 1991 offer very little comfort . . .

2

I'm here today to report our findings and to present a series of options to help you to formulate an appropriate strategy for the present hostile environment. I've divided up my presentation as follows.

Firstly, I'd like to look at the factors which have influenced Visitron's historical performance. Secondly, I want to analyse the current business situation. Thirdly, I'm going to present the options which we see open to us and then, finally, I shall be recommending a corporate strategy for the 1990s.

Right. Let me begin by putting the current difficulties into some kind of perspective.

3

I'd like you to look at this graph. Here we can see a fairly typical growth-curve for a company first in the field in a new high-tech industry . . . turnover rising dramatically in the early growth phase, flattening out in the face of competition, and then recovering as we responded to that competition.

Visitron's early success was due to three main factors. Firstly the company was protected by patents. Secondly there was the vital UK Government contract in 1965, here on the graph, and thirdly the direct-selling policy was extremely successful. We can trace the beginning of Visitron's problems to the end of the patents in 1972. Kamakura entered the market in that year with Large and Medium Unit machines, and was followed a year later by Hyperscan with the first Small Unit models. The story after that is familiar to all of us . . .

Faced with severe price competition and very good 'me too' product, Visitron's market shares declined and profitability slumped. The 1975 Company Plan was the first attempt to climb back. In a nutshell, the strategy was to win back market shares by establishing an unbeatable technological lead. R&D was doubled, and later that year Visitron launched its first Small Unit machine.

4

I think we should be frank, ladies and gentlemen. The 1975 plan was only partially successful. You will note that, although sales picked up, they have never again approached the rate of growth of the overall market.

The reason for this, as I think we all know, is that since the mid-70s the fastest growing sector of the market has been the Small Unit sector, and Visitron has consistently failed to increase its initial foothold in this sector.

If we look at the overall market, we can see that the Small Unit sector has grown from 25 per cent in 1981 to 41 per cent this year. Over the same period, Visitron's share of that sector has fallen from 20 per cent to 11 per cent.

It would seem, then, that the 1975 Plan failed to get to the root of the problem. Technical lead has not been enough to restore our position in the market . . . Other factors have been working against Visitron, and since the beginning of this year the factors have become critical. In 1986, trading profits have dropped below the three million mark, and now represent only 1.3 per cent of turnover . . . So what has gone wrong?

5

I'd like to try and answer the question by analysing the current business situation from two angles: first price, then cost.

Have a look at this diagram. This is an index of scanner prices from 1980 to 1986 with a projection to 1991. The vertical axis represents the indices of scanner prices over that period, with 1980 as the base year. The horizontal axis shows the years 1980 to 1991. The solid line, here, indicates scanner prices in the Small Unit sector and the broken line prices in the Medium Unit sector.

As you see, prices in the Small and Medium Unit sectors have been falling steadily since the early '80s as a result of severe competitive pricing. This is bad enough, but the new factor in the picture is here: Hyperscan entered the Large Unit sector six months ago with an aggressive pricing strategy which has caused heavy defensive discounting throughout this sector. We were slow to react, and the result is that we are now in danger of losing the dominant position in our most lucrative market. If you need evidence of this, look at these diagrams of comparative market shares.

6

In 1981 we had dominant positions in the Large Unit sector – large hospitals and engineering companies – and the Medium Unit sector – middle-sized hospitals and firms. Since the middle of 1981, however, those shares have been eroded by 9 per cent and 4.5 per cent respectively – figures which seem to correspond exactly to specific dips in the price indices over that period. You will also see that since our very satisfactory 20 per cent penetration of the Small Unit sector – doctors' surgeries and small firms – in 1981, this slice has slumped to 11 per cent. And our current forecasts show that it will shrink to 6 per cent by 1991.

Our expectations are almost as gloomy in the Large and Medium sectors. If you now look at overall market share, you can see that Visitron's share is 16 per cent lower than in 1981 whereas Kamakura's is 1 per cent lower and Hyperscan's is 17 per cent higher. I think the figures speak for themselves.

I should also say in passing that we are considerably over-dependent on government contracts in the Large Unit sector. The 9 per cent fall in sector share only hints at a much more serious danger – the always possible loss of government business. I shall be suggesting a way to sidestep this nightmare scenario in due course.

7

Right, ladies and gentlemen. Those are the symptoms. Let's now move on to an examination of Visitron's cost situation and general internal condition.

If you refer to this bar chart, you will see the trading positions in our three divisions in 1986. You can see immediately that our trading profits have come almost entirely from our Large Unit division, whereas our Medium Unit division has only just managed to break even.

The Small Unit division, however, has been the major drain on cash, recording a £3 million loss over the year. A combination of sales target shortfalls and budget overruns – particularly in the area of sales and distribution and manufacturing payroll – seems to have been the main cause of this situation. In our Large Unit division hard prices protected us till mid '86, but with respect to the other divisions, the cost escalations have been disastrous.

8

We don't think that you can blame last year's strike entirely for the rise in the wage bill – the figures are not much above the national trend – but the long-term consequences for Visitron are clear from the latest figures for return on capital employed. This figure here currently stands at 2.5% which, as you will notice, is 11% below the industry average, here . . . Our ability to attract new investors or to borrow from normal sources is being threatened, and the present falling share value could lead to a serious takeover risk.

So, with hindsight, it now seems clear that the 1975 decision to go simply for a technological lead resulted in a corporate facelift but did not tackle our underlying manufacturing problem. We maintained our technical image in the market, but we had put on too much manufacturing fat during the good years. In the hostile climate of the '70s we could not compete on prices, and the market, ladies and gentlemen, found us out. Our findings show that customers in all sectors now consider our marginal technical superiority is not worth paying the 'image premium' associated with the name Visitron.

They want lower prices. And, ladies and gentlemen, they can get them – but not from us!

Let me digress for a moment. During our fact-finding discussions within the company it was suggested – in some quarters – that Visitron should pull out of the Small Unit sector altogether and leave it to the so-called

'Mickey Mouse' operators. The reasons given were simple. First, our profits come from the other two sectors, and secondly it is impossible to reduce our production costs to the level of our overseas competitors. Again there seemed to be a wish to retreat to the comfortable position of the early years. We have, however, considered this point of view very carefully, and I shall come to our conclusion in a moment.

Anyway, let me get back to my main argument.

9

Price has become the key competitive weapon in all sectors of the market. In the Small Unit sector this has been the case since 1980. Unless we can reduce our prices there by at least 10%, we will be squeezed out of this sector very quickly.

In addition to this, however, we must expect further sharp price falls in the Medium and Large Unit sectors over the next five years. We only have to look at the launch of the Hyperscan Large Unit machine recently to see what this means for Visitron. Hyperscan's price undercut ours by 25% and this has given them 9% of the market in six months.

What I am getting at is that in the last ten years there has been a certain loss of corporate vision in parts of this company. Ladies and gentlemen, for at least five years the market has been saying 'Give us price, not image!' – and we have ignored them.

Visitron has to become more market-oriented and give the customer what he wants. Unless we do this, our very survival will be at stake.

10

The obvious question is, can we reconcile two apparently conflicting aims? Firstly, to provide quality scanners at acceptable prices in a highly competitive market, and secondly, to raise the return on investment to attract investors?

It seems to us that we must look for two things. A short-term strategy to defend our present market position, and a long-term strategy to cut manufacturing costs and allow us to return to the offensive within five years. As far as the short-term strategy is concerned, union resistance and the national trend in labour costs make it impossible to reduce our manufacturing costs in the near future. This means that our only immediate source of cost savings will be in sales and distribution. But can we achieve these savings and increase sales at the same time?

We have taken careful note of the Marketing Division's views on this subject, but on the basis of the results from the recent sales area test of the dealer franchise system, we are inclined to be more optimistic than they are.

Before I go on to this, I would like to put forward the corporate targets which will have to be achieved if Visitron is to ensure its future.

Our major long-term target can be stated quite simply. By 1995 we must restore return on capital employed to the industry average of 13.5%. To do this we must hold our current market shares for the immediate future, then increase them to their original level by the early '90s, and achieve a 25% reduction in costs in real terms by 1991. Finally we must reduce our dependence on government business, especially in the Large Unit sector.

11

This brings me to the final part of my presentation here this morning.

Using this product spread matrix, I'd now like to present the options we see open to Visitron in the current situation. Very briefly, the matrix shows our present spread of products in terms of market growth, on the vertical axis, and relative market share on the horizontal axis. Our two established products, our Medium and Large Unit machines, are down here in the highly profitable cash cow quadrant – still, for the moment, generating cash to keep us afloat. But here, in the top right-hand quadrant, we have our Small Unit product with a very small share of a rapidly growing market sector. Our present low sector share and the negative profitability on this product put a very large question mark against its future. In Option A we would pull out of this sector altogether for the reasons given earlier. If we did this we would enjoy immediate savings in the region of £4m per annum.

The survey I mentioned earlier, however, suggests there would be important hidden costs in this option. The major finding was that 20 per cent of our new customers in the Large and Medium Unit sectors since 1975 have been upgraded from Visitron Small Unit machines. It would seem, ladies and gentlemen, that our so-called 'down-market' product has been responsible for a much larger chunk of our 'serious' business than conventional wisdom suggests.

Furthermore, since 40 per cent of the components in the Small Unit range are common to the other machines there is quite a large contribution to overheads from this range. We therefore estimate that the true savings from Option A may be as small as £½m annually.

12

To consider Option B we must look again at the overall matrix. Every company needs its cash cows – high market shares in low-growth markets, with very high profitability. For years now our Large and Medium Unit products have been our cash cows. Now, however, they are under threat. The Medium Unit product is already moving towards negative profitability, and this year the Large Unit product has begun to shift in the same direction. The most worrying thing, however, is the absence of any Visitron product here, in the top left quadrant, where we should find future highly profitable products in the pipeline. It is in this area that we ought to be looking for our long-term profitability. At the moment the cupboard is bare. In Option B, therefore, we would stay in all three sectors of the market but identify the Small Unit sector as our major growth area – in other words push our Small Unit product into this quadrant . . . We would do this by employing a market segmentation strategy, offering the present Small Unit machine 5% above its current price, but also offering a stripped-down version which undercuts this by 20%. This new price system would be partly financed by an immediate change-over to a dealer-franchise system in the Small Unit sector.

Yes, it will mean job losses – but since this option will also include a sales drive in the Large Unit sector to reduce our over-dependence on government contracts, redundancies would be minimised by the transfer of our best salesmen to the Large Unit Division.

Finally, ladies and gentlemen, Option B would also include a re-launch of the Small Unit product range to coincide with the start-up of the new dealer-system.

Now for the long-term options. To achieve the 25% reduction in costs by 1991, Option C proposes relocating our main production centres to low labour-cost areas abroad. Option D is perhaps a more imaginative solution. Kamakura is also having problems in the Small Unit sector, due mainly to the tariff barriers of the EEC. If Kamakura and Visitron pooled production resources in the UK to produce a common Small Unit machine – remaining in competition in the other sectors, of course – there would be advantages for both sides. Kamakura would get inside the tariff wall. We would gain their expertise – and their dealer network. Option D is described in full in our *Proposals to management*, which I shall hand out after this presentation.

13

Right. To conclude my presentation, I'd now like to outline our recommendations. I've divided them into the short-term operational plan and the long-term investment plan. First, the operational plan.

Because of the need for high-growth, high-profit potential products, and because of the interdependence of all three sectors of the market, we reject Option A. Withdraw from the Small Unit sector and you can say goodbye to growth. No, ladies and gentlemen, Option B is the only way forward. It will require new, aggressive marketing in this company, but it will buy time for us while the long-term plan is put into motion. The franchise test project produced very good results which, if extrapolated to the whole market, would cut sales costs sufficiently to allow price reductions of up to 20 per cent and improve our sector share to about 18 per cent.

As far as the long-term investment plan is concerned, we strongly urge that feasibility studies be carried out into both options. The results should be available to management by the middle of next year for a decision by the end of 1987.

Our final proposal is for an accelerated R&D. programme to be included in the Investment Plan, so that by 1991 we will have re-stocked our empty cupboard with a new range of products which will give us total, effective market coverage in the 1990s.

Ladies and gentlemen, these are our proposals. I should add that my colleague, Mr Turnbull, will be presenting the financial implications of these recommendations at this afternoon's session. But now let me give you our five-year planning map to 1991. It would look something like this:

We introduce the dealer-franchise system immediately. At the same time we phase in the new Small Unit strategy. The Small Unit range will be re-launched in July next year. By 1988 work could begin on our new low-cost plants either abroad or in the UK. By 1990 those plants would come on stream.

14

To sum up then . . . Visitron must become more market-oriented if it is to survive. Our main competitor, Hyperscan, can no longer be dismissed as the 'Mickey Mouse' operator of past years. Mickey Mouse, ladies and gentlemen, has already become Mighty Mouse, and this year we have watched him nibble away a slice of our prime market. Next year we expect him to bite hard. Only a radical reorganisation of our manufacturing base and a complete range of highly competitive, top-quality products by 1990 will ensure our survival to the year 2000.

I'd like to conclude, ladies and gentlemen, by reminding you of something your Chairman said in the highly successful early days of this company. He said – correct me if I'm wrong, Sir David – he said there are three kinds of companies. There are those that make things happen, those that watch things happen, and those that wonder what happened! Ladies and gentlemen, if Visitron is to survive to the year 2000 we must start to make things happen now!

Thank you. You no doubt have many questions, so . . .

Valerie Singleton

Well, there it is – things looked pretty bleak for Visitron but now they don't seem quite so bad.

I wonder . . . what *does* the future hold now for Visitron?